THE PURSUIT
OF WILD TROUT

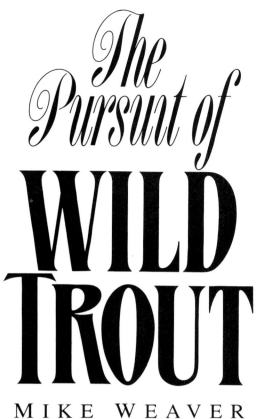

The Pursuit of
WILD TROUT

MIKE WEAVER

MERLIN UNWIN BOOKS

First published in Great Britain by Merlin Unwin Books, 1991

Published by:
MERLIN UNWIN BOOKS, 20 MONTPELIER GROVE,
LONDON NW5 2XD

Trade distribution by:
CHRIS LLOYD SALES AND MARKETING SERVICES

BRITISH LIBRARY CATALOGUING IN PUBLICATION DATA

Weaver, Michael
    The pursuit of wild trout.
    I. Title
    799.1755

    ISBN 1-873674-00-7

Designed by Colin Lewis
Typeset in 11/13 point Linotype Caledonia (Cornelia) by Nene Phototypesetters Ltd, Northampton
and printed in Great Britain by Butler and Tanner Ltd, Frome.

ACKNOWLEDGEMENTS

Anyone who writes a book on fishing could list dozens of fellow anglers, fishery owners and others who have helped directly or indirectly to make it possible. The demands of space make it possible to mention but a few.

My thanks go the late Harry Sealey of Cheltenham who first encouraged me to take up fly fishing; to Sid Neff, who has influenced my fly fishing for river trout more than any other angler; to Richard Slocock for access to his lovely Dorset streams for testing techniques and flies, photography and, of course, fishing.

My writing has received constant encouragement from the editors of *Trout & Salmon* who have published my articles through more than twenty years – Jack Thorndike, Roy Eaton and Sandy Leventon. In particular, my thanks go to Sandy Leventon for permission to use in this book some passages that have previously been published in *Trout & Salmon*. I am also grateful to the other editors who have published my work over the years in both magazines and the books to which I have contributed; especially Chris Dawn (*Trout Fisherman*, in which part of the chapter on the Lyn was published), Brian Harris (who used my first ever article in the long-departed *Angling*), Dennis Bitton (*The Flyfisher*, USA), Anne Voss Bark (*West Country Fly Fishing*), David Barr (*The Haig Book of Trout Fishing in Britain*) and Peter Lapsley (*The Complete Fly Fisher*). And, of course, to Merlin Unwin, who made me find the time to write this book, gave me unstinting help throughout its preparation and then published it.

And finally my wife, Linda. It is customary for the authors of angling books to thank their wives for their tolerance and making them welcome when they come home wet, muddy and smelling of fish. My gratitude to Linda goes far beyond that, as she took all of the pictures in this book in which I feature, and typed the complete manuscript. To say that without her this book would not have been produced is no more than a statement of fact. To her this book is dedicated.

CONTENTS

INTRODUCTION

ARLY SPRING DAYS in the middle of March can be distinctly chilly and this day was no exception. I had arrived at the river by ten o'clock, tackled up and was now working down a gravel run with a team of wet flies. For a couple of hours there was little sign of any life in the river, with only several salmon parr coming to my Greenwell's Glory. Then, just around noon as a watery sun raised the temperature a degree or two, a few little dark flies emerged and drifted down on the quick current. Even in my state of innocence and inexperience, I knew that they were dark olives and quickly tied on a single dry Rough Olive that I had bought a few days earlier. By the time I had changed my fly, the number of duns had increased and the surface was broken in several places by the rises of fish. After several attempts I managed to place the Rough Olive reasonably close to one of the rises. It drifted downstream for a foot and suddenly it was sucked in and I was playing a brown trout of about half a pound.

Not only was that the first trout of the day but also my first ever river trout on a fly. The place was the River Usk at Glangrwyney and the year was 1960. Although I had already caught much bigger trout on fly from Chew and Blagdon, that modest brown was undoubtedly a turning-point and led gradually to fly fishing for trout in running water becoming my main preoccupation as an angler – a preoccupation that has remained with me ever since, even though I fish for other species and occasionally with methods other than fly.

I was perhaps fortunate that my early river fishing was on the streams along the Welsh Marches, where the association and other permit waters on the Usk, Monnow, Lugg and Arrow were within an easy drive of my home. Few of the stretches that I fished were stocked and many had a healthy head of wild fish, so quite soon I developed a taste for catching these naturally propagated fish on rough wild streams.

Like most anglers, I also enjoyed taking home my catch for the table and, I suspect, to gain the admiration of family and friends. But even in those early days I began to question the sense of killing wild trout, and to ask myself if by taking my full quota of fish home I was destroying my future sport. It was

particularly on a stretch of the Monnow at Skenfrith, controlled by the Birmingham Anglers' Association, that I began to see the need for restraint. It was obvious that the head of trout on this very pleasant fishery was far from prolific and, although I had never heard of catch-and-release or no-kill in those days, it seemed natural and indeed sensible to return all of my trout to maintain what breeding stock there was. Yet there were other anglers taking away the few trout that they caught, an act which seemed contrary to their own best interests.

From that initial decision on the Monnow it was only a matter of time before virtually all of my wild trout were being returned alive. That, for better or worse, is a theme that runs throughout this book. Inevitably, I will be accused of moralizing. However, my commitment to releasing wild trout is not a moral issue but purely one of self-interest. I have no compunction about killing fish and frequently do so on stocked lakes and pools where the trout are introduced to provide sport for anglers and then to be killed and eaten. But on any stream capable of sustaining a head of wild trout I cannot comprehend why anglers should want to kill them and replace them with fish from a hatchery. That seems to me to be a very poor bargain. So, although you will see plenty of pictures of fish in this book, you will see no pictures of dead trout.

If you decide to return your catch you will, I am afraid, be faced with a problem of credibility. In spite of the declared indifference to fishing expressed by a large sector of the population, who cannot wait to tell you that they would never have the patience to fish, most people seem to have an extraordinary interest in fishermen. As soon as they see you carrying a rod, they insist on rushing up and asking you what you have caught. When you tell them, the next request is to see the catch, and when you explain that you have returned five, ten, or twenty extremely edible trout the response is inevitably a glazed look of disbelief. All they have heard about fishermen being liars must be true!

It is easy to see how a novice angler would be troubled by this scepticism, but I was surprised when a famous angler of vast experience wrote after fishing a famous no-kill fishery in a foreign land that 'The bag at the end of the day has been for me the definitive statement of what you have caught. Unless you are fishing together as a party, you hesitate with catch-and-release to state the numbers you have taken on a good day, in case of disbelief.' My reaction to that is that I go fishing for my own satisfaction and pleasure. If my response to an enquiry about my catch is met with disbelief, it is a matter of total indifference to me.

Although I very occasionally visit mountain lakes which still hold wild trout, most of my lake fishing is on waters which are stocked regularly, so the fish have rarely had a chance to become really wild. This book, therefore, addresses itself chiefly to river fishing, where the angler seeking wild trout is most likely to find what he is looking for. I must confess also that since catching that first trout on the Usk I have gained greater enjoyment from fishing running water rather than lakes and reservoirs.

If you are looking for instruction on how to catch big trout and where to find them, read no further. I enjoy catching big fish as much as anyone, but size for me has become increasingly relative over the years. I was perhaps fortunate in starting my fly fishing for trout at Chew Valley in the fabulous days after its opening, so I managed to get any preoccupation with big fish out of my system at an early stage. The efficiency of fish farms in rearing rainbows to huge sizes has tended to distort the picture and, for me, the ultimate travesty was reading an article about a fishery in southern England that made the proud boast that it was stocking with record rainbows. What meaning or validity can there be in such a record?

The exploring angler who sets out in search of wild trout has a wonderful world of rivers and streams set out before him, but to enjoy it to the full you must be able to judge each water on its merits. Long ago I made the mental leap that enabled me to gain as much enjoyment from a half-pounder on a moorland stream or a two-pounder on a chalk stream as I would from a six-pounder on a reservoir. Once you have made that leap, the varied world of wild trout waters is yours to enjoy. In this book I have set out the methods which have proved successful on such waters and given me endless enjoy-ment – and I hope I have also provided a taste of those streams where I have found wild trout.

1

THE WILD TROUT

WHAT IS A wild trout? A century ago such a question would have had little meaning, as virtually all trout were truly wild. Since then, however, decades of increasing angling pressure, with the cropping of trout exceeding the ability of many rivers to replace them naturally, has resulted in widespread stocking with hatchery fish and the inevitable dilution of the natural strain.

Fortunately, even in these crowded islands, genuine untainted stocks still remain in many areas. The more mountainous and hilly parts of Scotland, Wales, Ireland and the north and south-west of England all have tumbling streams where the trout are so prolific that there has never been any need to consider artificial stocking. In the remoter parts of these areas there also remain lakes where the original strain of trout has remained intact.

For the absolute purist, only such trout can be considered truly wild, and most of us have to settle for something less pure most of the time. Does it really matter anyway? Some of the best fishing I have enjoyed has been the end result of introducing new species which have had the opportunity to become naturalized over many years, whether rainbow trout on a Derbyshire stream or brown trout in the Rocky Mountains of America.

Wildness in trout is more a state of mind in the angler – the feeling that you are enjoying a genuine natural experience pitting your wits against a really wild creature rather than a fish that may have had its last feed in a stewpond only hours ago. So even if the fish that I catch started its life in a hatchery, provided it has had plenty of time to acclimatize and become wild I may well enjoy an experience that is indistinguishable from catching a genetically pure wild brown trout. If its education has been increased and its fear of man sharpened as a result of its being caught and released along the way, so much the better. For me the object of the exercise is to enjoy as wild an experience as can be expected in the water I am fishing – whether the result of environmental factors or enlightened fishery management – without worrying too much about genetic purity.

ABOVE A cutthroat trout from Nelson's Spring Creek, Montana, showing the vivid slash of colour that gives it its name.

RIGHT A 4lb rainbow trout from Henry's Fork, Idaho, caught by George Anderson (see page 179).

Brown trout from the River Piddle in Dorset.

The brook trout is really a char.

BROWN TROUT

Where then should we be looking for wild trout in these islands? Our native brown trout, *Salmo trutta*, probably survives in most counties of the land, but in the flatter or more industrialized areas its hold is tenuous. What little stream fishing remains in the home counties is on closely guarded fisheries and likely to be artificial. Through East Anglia and much of the Midlands a similar situation pertains. In England you really need to travel west to Wessex and north to Derbyshire before you begin to find river trouting on a reasonable scale.

The great strongholds of the wild, or near-wild, trout in England are the south-west, especially Devon, and the northern counties of Yorkshire,

Cumbria, Northumbria and parts of Durham and Lancashire. The lovely limestone country of the Peak District has some of England's loveliest trout streams.

Except in the most urban and industrial areas, brown trout are everywhere in Wales and Scotland, though they often hold a subsidiary position to salmon. Nevertheless, there are rivers which have a reputation for trout in their own right, such as the Usk in Wales or the Don in Scotland.

Although the brown trout is a European species, it is now widespread and established through much of the temperate world, thanks to transplantation by man which started in the late nineteenth century. And the same variety that we see in our native fish is reflected in the stocks that have developed elsewhere in the world. I can recall taking big heavily spotted brown trout on a limestone stream in Montana which are of the same infinitely variable species as a dark little fish on an acid river in the Falklands.

The ability of the brown trout to become established in a new environment, reproduce itself and then survive has been demonstrated in many lands. When angling pressure has resulted in the native species being fished out on some American rivers, electric fishing has still revealed a good head of brown trout which have resisted all efforts to catch them.

RAINBOW TROUT

And then there is the rainbow trout, *Salmo gairdneri*, whose presence in British rivers is something of a vexed question. It first arrived from America about a century ago but, unlike the case in other countries, it has been almost uniquely unsuccessful in establishing itself – the Wye in Derbyshire being the notable exception. With so many stillwater fisheries being stocked with rainbows and countless hatcheries throughout the country, rainbows are constantly escaping into rivers, but fail to produce any stream-bred fish, even though browns reproduce perfectly satisfactorily in the same streams. Probably these rainbows are so many generations removed from native stock that they no longer know how to go about reproduction without help from man.

There is a tendency among many anglers to decry the rainbow, perhaps because most anglers catch rainbows that are fresh from the hatchery, with the worn-down fins and scruffy scales that rearing in such crowded conditions often produces. Somehow the brown is thought to be a cut above the rainbow, but are they comparing like with like? A moorland reservoir near my home stocks with large browns and describes the result as 'quality brown-trout fishing', but the stocked fish quickly go back in condition and offer no more of a quality experience than did the rainbows that were stocked there before. The fact is that a wild stream-bred rainbow is a magnificent fish.

Although most river authorities are opposed to the introduction of rainbows, there are many rivers that I fish where I would love to see a natural stock of this species. Rainbows are great food converters and I can think of many acid streams where anything that would increase the average fish by an ounce or two would be welcome. But here I have ventured into heresy and I can almost feel the flames licking at my feet. I suspect that during my lifetime I will have to continue to enjoy wild rainbow fishing on the odd trip to Derbyshire or America.

Like the brown trout, the rainbow too has been taken to many parts of the world from its original home on the Pacific coast streams of North America. The range of the rainbow now includes other parts of the United States and Canada, Patagonia, New Zealand, Australia, Europe and South Africa. There are even pockets of rainbows in the tropics, as in Kenya, where the mountains bring the temperature down to an acceptable level. In many of these places, genuine wild stocks have become established and provide splendid sport for the angler.

B R O O K   T R O U T

The other trout that I have enjoyed catching in its wild state is not a trout at all but a char – the brook trout, *Salvelinus fontinalis*. In its native eastern United States its range has been drastically reduced, as its demands for cool and pure water are greater than the browns and rainbows that have often replaced it. But it too has been transported to new habitats. High in the Centennial Valley on the continental divide in Montana I enjoyed catching colourful little brookies on a day off from the serious fishing on the more famous rivers. The biggest brook trout that I have met so far was back in its native habitat on the Roach River in Maine. It was at the end of a day with the landlocked salmon in September when a big fish took my streamer and bore deep into the pool, unlike the jumping landlocks that I had been catching. Eventually that stubborn fish came to the net and I was left admiring a magnificent cock brook trout in its spawning colours. The tape said twenty inches, so I guessed it at three pounds before slipping it back into the river.

2
PROTECTING THE FUTURE

'YOU CAN'T HAVE your cake and eat it too' is an old saying that applies with particular relevance to wild trout. As more and more anglers want to fish for trout in an ever more crowded world, the only hope of hanging on to our wild stocks is to adopt conservation measures that traditionalist anglers, used to carrying home a bag of fish, may find difficult to accept.

Is there any real alternative if we are to preserve the priceless asset of wild trout in our streams? If too many anglers kill too many fish, the result is poorer sport for the real fisherman, whichever way you look at it. Overkill without remedial action will simply result in dangerously reduced stocks and fisheries that have little appeal to the angler. The traditional remedy has been restocking, but on a wild-trout fishery that can easily make matters worse if the introduction of too many hatchery fish tips the balance against the native population. We can end up with the ultimate travesty – catching only domesticated stocks on a natural stream perfectly capable of sustaining a wild stock. It can happen and indeed has happened.

Streams denuded of trout or populated only by hatchery fish are, of course, the extreme and still the exception. The real tragedy is the large number of rivers where the ecosystem is still basically sound yet the wild-trout fishing is but a shadow of what it could be. It always saddens me when I travel to a stream which is perfectly capable of reproducing and sustaining a large head of trout, only to experience mediocre fishing. The acceptance of a degree of restraint would probably result in a dramatic improvement in the fishing.

BAG LIMITS

There is nothing new in setting a limit on the number of fish that we kill and bag limits have a long and honourable tradition. There is the very small bag limit which permits the angler to kill, say, four trout, after which fishing must cease. Such tight limits are usually imposed on fisheries that have virtually ceased to hold wild fish and are dependent on stocked trout. Sadly, this applies to many stretches of our most famous chalk streams, which is the

Gently hold the fish, nose to the current, until it swims away.

reason why I make little effort to fish them. Why anyone should want to make a long trip at considerable expense to catch four hatchery trout is beyond me.

On the rivers of mountains and moorland, bag limits are usually far more generous – often eight, ten, or even a dozen fish. As these streams remain pure and frequently offer optimum spawning conditions, it can be argued that killing such limits has little effect on the prolific stocks of trout. The problem is that the constant killing of limit bags of keepable trout results in the reduction of stocks of the very trout that are most desirable to the angler. So, if a wild-trout fishery is to achieve its full potential, something more than the imposition of generous bag limits is needed.

It was perhaps inevitable that in the United States, the country above all others where they thought that nature was inexhaustible, anglers first came to realize that if you wished to preserve wild-trout fishing of any quality the killing would have to stop. The boom in disposable income and leisure time after the Second World War resulted in more and more people turning to fishing – and in particular to trout fishing. Ever-increasing demand meant more and more stocking as wild populations were exhausted, and on many streams an army of meat fishermen caught many of the trout almost before the hatchery truck was over the horizon. By the fifties and sixties it had become necessary to carry out heavy stocking even on many rivers in the remoter parts of the West.

CATCH AND RELEASE

Fortunately, increasing numbers of enlightened anglers and fishery managers realized that their heritage of wild-trout fisheries was rapidly vanishing and the result was the gradual growth of what we now know as 'no-kill' or 'catch-and-release' fisheries. As such measures have spread, more and more rivers have clawed their way back towards their former glory and now offer anglers the opportunity to enjoy fishing of a quality that had been absent for decades.

The cycle of a river declining from once-great fishing to mediocrity and then recovering to provide excellent fishing for an ever greater number of anglers was summed up by the American writer Charles E. Brooks in his book *The Trout and the Stream*, published in 1974. He was writing about Yellowstone National Park, and in particular about the Yellowstone River, where stocking of hatchery trout was stopped in 1958 and no-kill regulations came into effect in 1962, after the quality of fishing had declined drastically. He wrote:

> I have fished Yellowstone Park waters since 1947, when the fishing was unbelievably good. I noted the decline in fishing and the increase in angling pressure, and made the obvious conclusion. Since the new regulations went into effect, I have observed the conditions very closely. Last year the Yellowstone was nearly as good fishing as it was in the late forties. Fish from twelve to fifteen inches ranged the stream in unbeliev- able numbers, and in a day's fishing, a few of sixteen and seventeen inches came to net. There has been no change in the river ecosystem, there have been no climate changes from normal. One therefore has to assume that the new regulations have done the job they were intended to do.

Over the years I have had the good fortune to experience American trout fishing in states as far apart as Pennsylvania, Montana, Idaho, Wyoming and Arkansas, and to observe at first hand the effects of various kinds of legislation and management on the fishing. Regulations have varied from outright no-kill to the taking of a six-fish limit by any legal method, with a variety of measures between those extremes. On Henry's Fork in Idaho I could have killed anything *under* twelve inches, nothing between twelve and twenty inches, and one fish per day over that length – a policy clearly aimed at maintaining a stock of large trout. On the Firehole River in Yellowstone National Park the minimum takable size was sixteen inches with a bag limit of two. Although I caught and saw many other anglers catch fish that could have been kept on both Henry's Fork and the Firehole, I never saw a fish killed.

DELAYED HARVEST

Both of those rivers were more than capable of providing a self-sustaining stock of wild trout, given the right regulations, but in 1989 I visited a river in Pennsylvania where a different set of regulations provided trout fishing that was as near to natural as possible on a stream without the capability of providing its own stock of wild trout. Here the management technique was what is known as 'delayed harvest'. This was a mixed fishery, with bass and other warm-water species, with limited spawning areas for trout, yet it was a lovely-looking stream running through wooded country, with a series of riffles and pools, the quicker water ideal for trout and fly fishing. To provide the angler with trout fishing, the Pennsylvania Fish and Game Commission stock with trout at the beginning of the season and impose a no-kill rule until the end of June, after which the normal bag limit can be killed. The fishery managers have realized that after June the rising water temperatures would reduce the trout habitat to a few spring holes and cooler tributaries, and any surviving trout stocks would be severely reduced in the harsh winter, so anglers are permitted to kill a limit between June and the end of the season. The single pre-season stocking followed by catch-and-release means that the trout have the chance to become acclimatized and, as their days in the hatchery become more remote, increasingly they take on the mantle of wild fish. While this can never be true wild-trout fishing, it certainly comes very close and attracts many fly fishers who would never go near a stream that is constantly topped up with scruffy stump-tailed trout from the hatchery truck.

Catch-and-release has been slow to catch on in Britain and Richard Slocock's Tolpuddle Trout Fishery on the Piddle and Frome is still the only river fishery that I am aware of where no-kill regulations are imposed. The outstanding fishing which these rules have created is dealt with in a separate chapter later in this book. Increasingly, more and more anglers are returning their trout when on a wild fishery, and the owners of fishing hotels such as the Arundell Arms and the Half Moon, both in Devon, tell me that probably a majority of their guests are now returning their wild trout alive, even if well over the size limit.

My own belief is that catch-and-release will increase rapidly in Britain as more and more anglers tire of catching hatchery trout and realize that a healthy stock of wild trout can be maintained only if most are returned alive. However, returning a trout to the stream is a complete waste of time if the trout quickly turns over and dies as a result of its encounter with the angler. The fly fisher who decides to return his trout must learn the tricks that ensure that it has every chance of survival.

BARBLESS HOOKS

The first and probably most obvious obligation is to stop using barbed hooks, either tying your flies on barbless hooks or flattening the barbs of hooks which have them. Barbless hooks are now readily available for those who tie their own flies and a pair of needle-nosed pliers can be used to crush barbs when necessary.

We have all grown up on stories of epic struggles over many minutes or even hours with big fish, and anglers often boast of how long it took them to subdue a fish. Such an attitude is acceptable in our days of innocence, but is totally out of place in an experienced angler. Even if you intend to kill a fish, there is little excuse for prolonging the time between hooking it and bringing it to the net; if a fish is to be returned alive, prolonged playing becomes even more of a nonsense. Biologists tell us that the longer a trout is played the more likely it is that the build-up of acid toxicity will reduce the chances of recovery and I am quite willing to accept their word for it. Trout can be played far harder than most anglers realize, even on fine tackle, so if you wish to impress others with your skill your boast should be of the speed with which you played your trout and then either killed it or – preferably, in the case of wild fish – slid it back into the stream.

Having subdued the trout, quick and efficient unhooking is essential and here I use two techniques. If the fish is small, up to say eight or nine inches, I leave it in the water, reach down and grasp the shank of the hook; normally the fish will quickly shake itself off the barbless hook. In the case of larger trout, I always use the landing net. Once the fish is in the net I hold it in my left hand, still in the net, remove the fly with the fingers of the right hand, and then slip the fish back into the water straight from the net. While in the net, trout can be held securely with far less pressure than is needed with the bare hand and suffer far less damage. Occasionally a trout will take the fly deeply and then the artery forceps which are always clipped to the flap on one of the pockets of my waistcoat are ready for instant use. With forceps and barbless hooks, the hook can even be retrieved from the gill filaments without drawing blood.

Even if you intend to kill a fish, there can be no excuse for prolonging the time between hooking it and tapping it on the head with a priest, or for handling it in an insensitive way. If, however, you are going to return it to the river to fight another day and perhaps produce more wild trout, the attention that you pay to returning it in the best possible condition is surely an example of both humane behaviour and enlightened self-interest.

ABOVE A seventeen-inch Piddle brown is held in the mesh of the landing net while the barbless hook is eased out.

LEFT Artery forceps are always useful when the fly is out of finger reach.

3

A DIFFERENT APPROACH

A CENTURY AGO, most trout fishermen would have started their fishing with wild fish. Since then, things have changed dramatically. Now the first trout most anglers are likely to meet is a fish that was introduced to the water only days and possibly hours earlier. The put-and-take stillwater fishery, where trout of takable size are stocked on virtually a daily basis, has become the norm for many anglers and these fisheries undoubtedly do a great job in providing readily available trout fishing for thousands of anglers, often in areas where none existed before.

The problem is that a rich diet of such put-and-take fishing can produce a very distorted view of fly fishing for trout in general, and particularly for wild trout on rivers. I meet many anglers on my local rivers who, although still enjoying their fishing on stocked pools, have started to feel that there is a bit more to life and have come to sample running water and wild brown trout. Things can quickly turn sour, however. They slip and slide on the rocky bottom; almost every back cast seems to find an overhanging branch; they hardly catch a trout and those that they do catch are only five or six inches in length. Many – perhaps a majority – rapidly become disillusioned, decide that this angling delight they had read about is closer to a nightmare, and return to the stocked pools with manicured banks, nothing to catch the back cast, and the virtual guarantee of large trout. 'Thank goodness, that's less pressure on our streams' might be the immediate selfish reaction, but I am always sorry to see someone turn away from the branch of our sport which has given me so much pleasure and excitement over the years.

To make the jump from freshly stocked trout to the wild fish you have to change both your attitude and tactics. On a lake you often hear someone saying, 'It's the fly in the water that catches the fish' – in other words, persistence pays. Once the fly is out there in the water working for you, then you are always in with a chance. It need not matter how it was presented, what it actually is, or how it is being fished – sooner or later, a recently introduced rainbow will come along and take it.

FIND THE FISH...

With the wild trout on the stream, this approach just does not work. Any trout worth catching has had to survive for several years, avoid predators, and find a position where it can obtain a steady food supply without expending too much energy. That means that, while you can stand in one spot on a stocked lake and have at least some expectation of a fish or two swimming by, on the stream you have to go looking for the trout. You must be mobile. So many anglers park the car, tackle up, walk to the first convenient spot and then start fishing. Such an approach on a trout stream is disastrous. It is far better to spend an hour or two walking the river and locating the fish, so that when you cast the first fly it has a chance of actually being seen by a decent trout.

Never forget that wild trout really are wild and scared stiff of a human being standing in full view. I know that you can stand virtually on top of stocked trout and still catch them, because I have frequently done so, but give a wild trout even an inkling that you are there and it is gone. So you need to use all the tricks of keeping off the skyline, approaching fish from downstream, and wading or walking quietly to get within casting range of the fish, and even then you will often frighten a previously unseen small fish which rushes up through the pool, frightening the trout you are really after.

...AND GIVE IT WHAT IT WANTS

By the time a wild trout reaches catchable size it will have eaten a lot of natural food over a lengthy period, and that means that it is unlikely to be very impressed by the colourful lures that are so attractive to rainbows straight from the stewpond. For consistent success you need to show the trout a suggestion or imitation of what it normally looks upon as food, so a working knowledge of those insects that trout feed upon is essential. Apart from the success it brings, understanding insect life and presenting your attempts to imitate it to the trout is what, for me, lifts this branch of fishing above all others.

If your fly-fishing apprenticeship has been spent on heavily stocked waters, there are many other ways in which your whole approach to fishing has to change if you are to achieve consistent success with wild trout on rivers. Any stocked fishery has to impose a tight bag limit if it is to avoid bankruptcy – probably four on a small pool and six on a reservoir, with fishing to stop as soon as the limit has been reached. Such limits, essential though they are, create an artificial situation and make it difficult to fish long enough and catch enough trout to learn from experience, except over a long period.

AN AMBITIOUS APPROACH

On a more natural water, where you can often catch and release as many trout as you like, you have ample opportunity to develop your technique in a short time. Unless I am visiting a stocked pool to get some trout for the kitchen, I have long preferred to fish those waters where I can catch and release trout until I have had enough, without my day being brought to an artificial close. There is nothing wrong with settling for a brace or two on a stocked fishery, but if you want to succeed on a natural stream with the wild trout a more ambitious approach is required.

On many stocked trout fisheries wading is not allowed, but if you are fishing a wild stream it becomes almost essential, and to get the best results that often means wading deep with full-length body waders. So forget any prejudice you have acquired about wading and get into the river with the fish – but do it quietly and carefully.

Remember that on a natural fishery the trout have seen it all before and have a strong instinct for survival, possibly honed by previous capture. On a stocked fishery, a trout's first mistake is likely to be its last, so few fish have the chance to develop the instincts that will keep them out of trouble. There are also some wild fisheries which are so remote or closely preserved that they hardly see an angler from one year to the next. Such waters, however, are beyond the reach of all but a few, and most of us have to fish on hotel, club and ticket waters, where there is likely to be a constant flow of anglers. Such fisheries may call for an apprenticeship which many anglers are unwilling to serve, but ultimately these are the fisheries that give lasting pleasure and satisfaction.

Autumn on the West Dart: spawning time for the wild stock.

4
FISHING THE RISE

*I*F I WERE asked to encapsulate the essence of fly fishing for trout in a single sentence, it would go something like this: 'Locate a steadily rising fish, identify the insect it is feeding on, present to the still rising fish an acceptable imitation, and then see the fish suck in the fly in the confident way that suggests it has been completely fooled.'

There is, of course, tremendous enjoyment to be derived from fly fishing without all of those ingredients being present, but the loss of any one of them somehow detracts from total satisfaction. I get great pleasure, for example, from working up a moorland stream and fishing each likely spot, but the anticipation as the fly approaches even the most enticing-looking lie is never quite the same as the exquisite excitement as a dry fly approaches a steadily rising trout. And tying on a standard pattern just because it has a reputation on the river being fished is a mechanical process compared with attempting to match the insect on which the trout are feeding.

So, whenever conditions make it possible, I fish a dry fly to rising trout, and this applies to rain-fed rivers as well as chalk and limestone streams. There is no sense of purity in this choice, which is based simply on the conclusion that, taking the season as a whole, the dry fly will catch more fish than other methods, and on many streams the better fish as well. And, above all, it is fun, which is the object of the exercise.

LOCATING THE FISH

Why should the dry fly be so effective, even though most trout on most rivers spend far more time taking food near the stream bed? I suspect that the simple answer is that by spotting a rising trout you have dealt with perhaps the biggest problem no matter what fish you are seeking – that of actually locating the fish. Also, the very act of rising demonstrates that a fish is feeding, so you have answered two of the basic questions of fishing in one go.

Fishing a floating fly to a rising trout can be ridiculously easy in certain conditions, and perhaps never more so than if you are on the river early in the season during a good rise to dark olives. Then, because no other fly is likely to be on the water, you know exactly what to tie on, the trout are rising in front of you, and after the rigours of winter they are far from choosy. Easy, you think, and so it is, but a few weeks later you may be out on a day when the flies are hatching and the fish are rising, but few are coming to your fly.

Late spring and early summer is usually a time of plenty, but you can be confronted with an embarrassment of riches. I recall a day in late May on the Suir in Ireland when things looked perfect, as indeed they were. Fish were rising everywhere to heavy hatches of fly, but I often found that my fly was being ignored. The problem was that several insects were hatching at the same time and it was necessary to identify which fly the trout were feeding on. A further problem was the fact that one trout would be feeding on, for example, the grey flag sedge, while another would be taking the iron blue.

Such days are the exception, but when they come you are offered both fly fishing at its most fascinating and the opportunity to catch a lot of fish. It is at such times that the angler with a basic knowledge of entomology can really cash in on the time spent learning to tell one insect from another.

And remember that things are not always what they seem. Many anglers will have experienced the classic example when a hatch of a substantial species such as the medium olive or olive upright appears to be exciting the trout yet no fish will take until you spot the presence of the inky little iron blues drifting down among the larger flies. A change to an imitation of the smaller insect will often prove to be the answer.

THE EMERGER

There are times, however, when there is clearly only one species hatching, yet your best presentation with a floating dun is ignored. Then the answer may be that the trout, although visibly rising, are taking the insects at the point of emergence. This can be particularly common with some of the smaller species of the Ephemeroptera such as pale wateries and small spurwings, which change very rapidly from nymph to dun and then leave the water almost instantly. The trout have little chance to take the winged insect but have plenty of time to take during the emergence itself. The importance of the emerger or floating nymph – call it what you will – was first brought home to me on Henry's Fork in Idaho and I have profited from the experience countless times since, particularly on chalk and limestone streams. Some tyings to imitate these emergers are given on page 58.

Once you have found a rising trout and identified what it is feeding on, you come to the final major challenge of presentation. There is no point in getting everything right up to that point and then putting the fish down with the very first cast. And always remember that it is that first cast that gives you the best chance of taking any rising trout. It is all too easy to become over excited by the sight of a rising trout and rush the first presentation. All can be lost. We are all guilty of this and I suppose that if we were not it would show that fly fishing no longer gave us a buzz. The trick is to reach a compromise between controlled excitement and restraint.

CASTING POSITION

When you spot a rising trout, think first about the best position to cast from. Your first instinct may be to throw a fly at the rise from where you are standing, but that can easily result in drag or the trout seeing the line before the fly. There are a few occasions when a natural insect moves independently of the current, but that is very much the exception. Most insects drift naturally on the current and that is what your artificial has to do.

Although it will be necessary from time to time to cast to a rise from every direction, the best position is usually across the river from the rise and from slightly downstream. In that way you minimize the risk of drag and keep

From across and slightly downstream...

the leader point away from the fish, provided that you do not cast beyond the rise. The fly is then dropped lightly on the surface, with a little slack line, a foot or two above the rise. The nearer the trout is to the surface, the closer the fly should be to the fish when it alights.

There will be many occasions when bankside growth, wind, depth of water, and other factors make it impossible to cast from the best position. Then it may be necessary to cast from directly downstream, or even from upstream. From immediately downstream it helps if a curve is thrown in the line, to keep the leader away from the fish, but this does take practice. A downstream cast with a dry fly can be very effective, as this is the best way of all to ensure that the trout sees the fly before the leader. However, drag becomes a very real problem, and it becomes necessary to cast with a very slack line. This can be achieved by casting high in the air and stopping the action, so that the line falls loosely on the water, with the rod still held high so that you can lower it as the line drifts away on the current. It sounds a bit complicated but is soon learned.

ABOVE Into a fish! The bankside reeds gave perfect cover for stalking this trout.

RIGHT October on the Dorset Piddle: casting to a rising fish in tricky, low water conditions.

CLOSE QUARTERS

Whichever direction you cast from, it always pays to get as close to the rising fish as conditions permit. Long casts take time, so the fly spends less time on the water. Short casts are likely to be more accurate and less sloppy, and the less line you have on the water, the less likely it is to be caught up in difficult cross currents. The best distance is probably between five and eight yards. You will be surprised at just how close you can approach a rising fish without putting it down, especially when wading with care.

If all goes well, up will come the trout and your fly will be absorbed. What do you do next? Instinct tends to take over, but it must be the right

instinct. Initially the tendency is to react violently, which can easily result in snatching the fly away from the fish, except with small trout in fast water, and we have all probably experienced five inches of trout flying past our ear. I have often tried to analyse exactly what I do and it can probably best be described as a steady raising of the rod tip, certainly no more than a gentle strike.

Fishing the rise can be both incredibly easy and maddeningly difficult, but it is always for me the most fascinating form of fly fishing and frequently the most successful. But, if you want to succeed with any degree of consistency, always remember the cardinal rule – make the first cast count.

5
FISHING THE WATER

A S MUCH AS I enjoy casting to trout that are rising or can be clearly seen, there are many occasions, especially on rain-fed rivers, when nothing is rising and it becomes necessary to fish the water. In doing so we immediately face several problems that do not occur in fishing the rise.

First of all, how do we know if the fish are actually feeding if there is no visual evidence? Then there is the question of location, which is made so easy by rising trout. And should we be fishing with a sinking or a floating fly?

Whilst we cannot know for sure if the trout are feeding until a fish actually takes the fly, it is possible to make some fairly intelligent guesses. Fish rarely feed well in extreme conditions, so it is best to avoid weather that is excessively hot or cold, and rivers that are in full flood or reduced to their bones by drought. Fortunately, in any conditions that can be described as reasonably normal, there will be at least some fish feeding, so there will be very few days over the course of a season when you cannot tempt a trout or two.

You will soon learn that even on the best waters trout are not evenly spread over the length of the river. Most novices learn this basic fact the hard way, by following their initial instincts to comb every inch of water. Eventually, this technique will produce the odd fish, because sooner or later the novice will reach water that holds fish, but much of the time he will be fishing over empty water or, at best, water that contains only small fish. Given sufficient time, and the ability to learn from experience, this method will build up a picture of where the better fish lie, but a lot of time will be wasted in the process.

BASIC REQUIREMENTS

To survive and prosper, trout need water that meets several basic requirements. These can be summarized as water temperature within the tolerable range, an acceptable level of dissolved oxygen, access to an adequate food supply, sufficient relief from fierce currents to avoid expending too much energy in holding position, and shelter to provide security from predators.

The first two requirements – temperature and oxygen – are likely to be reasonably constant due to the mixing effect of the current in a quick-flowing rain-fed river, but the other factors can be crucial in learning to spot those areas which are favoured by trout.

It is the current that brings food down to the fish and any concentration of the flow may well make a lie more attractive. A run between two weedbeds or two boulders will concentrate the flow of food, as will the outside of a bend if the current runs right against a steep or undercut bank. A fallen tree trunk will often act like a groyne and trout will lie along its upstream edge and especially where the current spills round the outside edge. If you are fortunate enough to be by the river on a day when there is a hatch of fly, you will see quite clearly how the floating insects are concentrated in these and other areas, and the information can be put to use when nothing is hatching.

The features that help to bring food to the trout will often also provide for the other two requirements – relief from the strongest currents and shelter from predators. A log or boulder which channels the flow of food also breaks the current and provides a useful bolt-hole when danger threatens.

HOLDING WATER

Many years ago I fished the River Dove in Derbyshire on a hot summer day when nothing was moving, until I allowed a nymph to be sucked by the undertow under one of the little limestone weirs. A good brown took immediately, the first of several more from similar spots, all of which provided oxygen, a supply of food and shelter.

So with practice it becomes possible to spot the holding water where trout, and especially the better than average fish, are to be found, without resorting to the trial and error of searching the whole river. These trout-holding features are not always easy to spot, especially on the larger rivers – and therein lies a basic rule for the newcomer to fishing the water. Your first efforts are more likely to be successful if they are made on a small stream, which will more readily reveal its secrets.

On a larger stream it is necessary to look for more subtle signs of where the trout are lying. The big, deep, glassy pools, where you can see the trout and they can see you, are a virtual waste of time, as are the broad stickles only a few inches deep, with cover only for tiny trout and salmon parr. It is something in between that you are looking for – water that is broken but not too turbulent, quick but not too rapid, and deep enough to provide security but not so deep that you cannot get down to the fish.

POCKETS AMONG THE BOULDERS

A broad piece of fast water which is studded with boulders is something to look out for on any medium-to-large stream, whether on Dartmoor or in the

ABOVE Early spring on the West
Dart: a boulder-strewn water
offering easy cover for the trout.

RIGHT Dry fly fishing on the
Upper Teign when there was a
brief hatch of dark olives.

Rockies. The trout can lie in the pockets of water between the boulders and feed, safe in the knowledge that cover is only inches away. This is also an advantage to the angler, as any trout that he frightens will dive under the nearest boulder, leaving the next little pocket undisturbed. On a big pool the fish would probably race upstream, ruining many yards of fishing.

Picking pockets on the East Lyn, Devon.

In the same way that it pays to spend time walking the river in search of rising trout, time spent exploring a new water and working out where the trout are likely to lie is never wasted. Intimate knowledge of a stream will tell you where fish are lying even if they are not showing. On my local River Teign, there are many places where I know almost to the inch where the better trout lie because I have caught fish from the same spots on many occasions over a long period. All rivers have such hot spots, and, the more you fish a stretch of water, the more you will accumulate this vital information. The keen anticipation experienced as your fly approaches one of these known lies is similar to that as a dry fly drifts towards a rising trout.

DRY OR WET?

The next decision is whether to fish with a floating or a sinking fly. In the first few weeks of the season, which probably starts in March on a rain-fed river, this is no problem, since the lack of hatches means that the trout will be finding more food close to the stream bed, and that is where your fly needs to be. On the smaller moorland streams, where the distance between surface and river bed is often only a foot or two, I use a couple of traditional wet flies such as the Half Stone or Blue Upright on a simple untapered leader, and fish them up, across or downstream as conditions permit. In the early days of the season, never worry about casting across and allowing the flies to swing round on the current; although it looks unnatural, this traditional method of fishing the wet fly is very effective when the river appears quiet.

On a big river, however, flies fished in this way are unlikely to be seen by trout lying on the bottom in four or more feet of water. To get the flies down you need a fast-sinking line or leader butt, with no more than four feet of nylon attached; there is no point in getting the line or butt near the bottom if the fly drifts up near the surface at the end of nine feet of nylon. A biggish Hare's Ear Nymph or Montana Nymph, with plenty of lead round the hook shank, will work well for this type of fishing.

Once the weather has warmed up and the trout have had their first taste of surface feeding, there is a real choice to be made between the floating and sinking fly. On small fast-flowing upland streams I change over to the floating fly by late April and then stay with it for the rest of the season, and I am sure that this is the key to more and better fish. There is nothing new in this; back in 1928, in his *Salmon and Trout in Moorland Streams*, Kenneth Dawson wrote: 'The dry fly has invaded the moorland and mountain streams which were once the inviolable sanctuary of the sunken lure, and there is no doubt in summer months that the former will at times kill far more fish, and those of considerably greater size, than could ever have been creeled by fishing wet.' Working your way up a moorland stream on a sparkling day in late spring or summer, casting a dry fly into all the likely spots, is one of the great pleasures of angling. My choice of fly for such a day would be a small hair-wing sedge, Grey Duster or Adams, size 16.

MEADOW STREAMS

On the clear moorland rivers I rarely use the nymph, simply because I have found the dry fly more effective, but on the slower, slightly coloured meadow streams the nymph has worked well for me when nothing has been showing. Allow a size 14 Pheasant Tail or Hare's Ear Nymph to sink in the slow current. The take will be marked by the leader sliding across the smooth surface.

The secret of fishing the water is choosing a stream that looks really interesting, with plenty of the features that offer clues to where the trout are lying. A smooth, featureless stretch of river can be very exciting when there is a big hatch of fly, but when nothing is moving such water is just plain boring.

6
TALKING ABOUT TACKLE

*F*ISHING FOR WILD trout is a mobile occupation and the more mobile you are the more fish you are likely to catch. Wild trout are rarely, if ever, spread evenly along a river, so it pays to move reasonably quickly from one productive spot to another. Particularly on rain-fed rivers when there is little surface activity, I frequently fish through two miles of river over the course of a morning, and that means that lightweight equipment and clothing is essential to avoid fatigue. Over the years my fly fishing outfits have evolved with that objective very much in mind. Fortunately, the development of modern fishing tackle has continuously taken us in the direction of ever lighter equipment, especially in the case of rods and reels, which have benefited from the use of new materials such as carbon fibre and magnesium.

But lightness is only part of the story. The job of a fly-fishing outfit is to put your fly exactly where you want it with the minimum of effort. Indeed, modern tackle is such that, once you have acquired the necessary casting skills, presenting a fly to a rising trout should be possible with hardly any conscious thought about the casting process. As long as you have to direct a significant part of your mental and physical efforts to casting the fly, you will always be struggling to get the best results.

Fishing equipment is inevitably a very personal choice and every fly fisher has to develop his own preferences and find the gear that is just right for him. I can only say that the equipment described in this chapter has worked well for me over many years and continues to do so.

A SELECTION OF RODS

Rod building has benefited enormously from the introduction of carbon fibre, which has brought the ownership of a high-tech, high-quality instrument within the reach of virtually every angler. In nearly forty years of fishing I have owned rods made of metal, greenheart, split cane and glass, but for the past decade I have used carbon fibre for all of my fly fishing.

My first carbon rod was acquired during a visit to the United States in 1977, when Sid Neff and I fished our way from Pennsylvania up to Maine and back again. He had obtained several Fenwick carbon blanks and at the end of

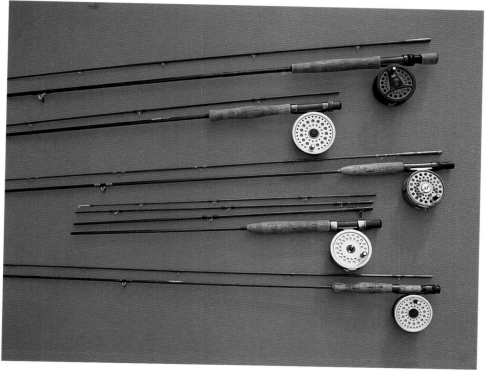

Five carbon rods to meet most river conditions: (top to bottom) 9½ft. Sage, 8½ft. Fibatube, 8½ft. Fenwick, 7½ft. Normark 4-piece, 7ft. Lamiglas.

the trip I returned with one of them, an 8½-footer for a No. 5 line. Over the following winter I assembled the rod in time for the 1978 season and I have been using it ever since on bigger rivers and on streams where I have to fish from the bank and need reasonable length to reach over bankside vegetation.

For wading the smaller streams, especially those where the trees reach out over the river, I had for some years been using a rod of 7 feet in glass, but had increasingly become aware of its lack of power and ability to cast a tight loop in confined spaces. The success of the Fenwick provided the obvious answer – a change to carbon fibre – and I selected a 7-foot Lamiglas blank for a No. 4 line. It was a fortunate choice and the resulting rod has since taken countless trout and remains as good as the day I assembled it in 1978.

Those two rods cater for virtually all my needs on the river, but there is always the possibility of loss or breakage so I have recently assembled a stand-in for the longer rod, this time based on a Fibatube blank. I will also have to look for a new model to back up the shorter rod, as the original Lamiglas blank is no longer manufactured. Fortunately, the range of carbon rods has grown to such an extent in the last decade that finding something similar should not be too difficult.

Occasionally something longer and more powerful is necessary, not so much for the trout but to cope with a big powerful river and the need to use heavy sinking lines and big leaded nymphs. On those rare occasions I use a 9½-foot Sage with a No. 7 line. I first used this outfit on a trip to the Falklands, when it coped easily with those southern gales, so I am unlikely to meet any conditions that will require a more powerful rod.

The most recent addition to my armoury is a travelling rod that breaks down into four pieces. For my long-range fishing trips I had always taken my usual rods protected by a reinforced rod carrier, but in 1990 I tagged on a few days fishing at the end of a business trip to the United States and that changed everything. All of my fishing clothing and tackle, including the rod, had to be packed in one duffel bag, which would have to accompany me through a week of business travel, often involving two flights a day. The only answer was a multi-piece rod but I certainly couldn't afford a Hardy Smuggler for only occasional use. The answer to my problem was the blank for a four-piece 7½-foot Normark Professional, which when broken down measures only 25 inches. Its first test was on the White River in Arkansas and my first sight of this big river made me wonder if the little rod would cope. Fortunately, it did, pushing a No. 5 line far enough out into the stream to produce some excellent fishing.

FLY LINES

When it comes to lines, I am something of an iconoclast. I have used the best lines that money can buy and I have used the cheapest – and I find it very difficult to tell the difference. A few years ago I was on a fishing trip with two editors from fishing magazines, one from Holland and the other from America. We were fishing big rivers in windy conditions and lines that would shoot smoothly into the breeze were at a premium. Both my companions were equipped with the latest that line technology could produce, while I was fishing with a fifteen-year-old slow-sinking mill end line, and after a few days fishing we all agreed that my cheap old line was the best of the lot. I realized, of course, that mine was probably a top-of-the-range line that had been discarded because of some minor defect in colour or length, but that experience brought home the fact that with a bit of luck you can acquire a range of first-class lines for remarkably little cost.

For most of my river fishing my needs are met by No. 4 and No. 5 lines, and whenever conditions permit I use the No. 4 to obtain the delicacy that the lighter line offers. In both sizes I use weight-forward lines, as so much of my fishing is at short range and with such a line plenty of weight is in the air even with a short cast. This, however, is purely a personal preference so if you would rather fish with a double-taper do not let me put you off. The double-taper line also offers the advantage of economy, as it can be turned round when one end becomes worn.

LEADERS

Whenever possible I use a floating line, whether for dry-fly fishing or for using the wet fly and nymph on shallow streams. Until quite recently I have usually carried spare reels with slow-sinking and fast-sinking lines for the odd occasions when I had to get down to the fish on big, deep rivers. Then came the trip to America which was tagged onto a business tour and weight restrictions which limited me to a travelling rod and only one reel. To keep the weight down I took the one reel filled with a WF5F line, but was able to fish at a variety of depths by using a range of braided tapered butts. Shortly before my trip, Airflo had sent me a sample of their trout leader set, which comprised five braided butts each 5 feet in length – floating, intermediate, slow-sinking, fast-sinking and super-fast-sinking. With the short length of plastic tubing supplied, I was able to change leaders to match the depth and speed of the stream while using just the one fly line.

Apart from the convenience, I enjoyed being able to stick with the floating line, even when bumping a big nymph along the bottom. I had never enjoyed using sinking lines on a river, feeling that a long length of line under water resulted in lack of control. Having most of the line at the surface, with only a short length dropping steeply to the sunk fly, somehow gives a real sense of being in touch, making both spotting the take and hooking the fish easier. Even with the little 7½-foot rod that I was using, the sinking butts cast smoothly, with only the super-fast sinker giving the 'lumpy' feel often experienced with sink-tip lines.

For the dry-fly fishing that accounts for most of my river trout fishing, I have been using floating braided butts since they were introduced. They proved to be an immediate success, being far more supple than the 20 lb breaking strain monofil butts that I used previously. At the other end of the leader – the point or tippet – there has been almost a revolution due to the relatively recent introduction of monofilaments that offer ever finer diameters for a given strength. Point material such as Super Strong from Orvis and Double Strength from Drennan have offered the fly fisher the opportunity to use finer points than ever before, a real advantage when presenting a fly to a suspicious wild trout.

For normal conditions I like to taper my dry-fly leaders down to a point with a strength of 2½ to 3 lb, which before the new materials meant a diameter of about 0·006 inch, distinctly on the coarse side under critical conditions. Now the same strength can be obtained at a diameter as fine as 0·004 inch, which is much more in keeping with a small dry fly. When conditions force you down to really tiny flies and even finer points, the fact that material as fine as 0·003 inch will still give a breaking strain of about 1½ lb makes ultra-fine fishing a sensible rather than foolhardy proposition.

Inevitably, handling such fine leader points calls for a light touch and matching tackle. A big powerful rod and a heavy line will result in a break almost every time, especially on the strike, so keep the rest of your gear in

LEADERS

These are the leaders that cover most of my needs, all produced with a combination of braided butt and nylon monofilament. You can, of course, purchase ready-made continuous-taper leaders, but making your own offers far greater flexibility, and the specifications I give here should be used as a basis which can be adapted to suit your own needs.

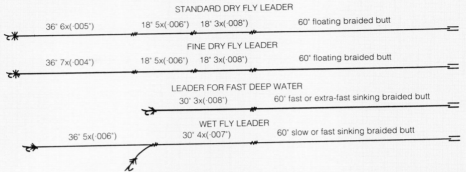

STANDARD DRY FLY LEADER
36" 6x(·005")   18" 5x(·006")   18" 3x(·008")   60" floating braided butt

FINE DRY FLY LEADER
36" 7x(·004")   18" 5x(·006")   18" 3x(·008")   60" floating braided butt

LEADER FOR FAST DEEP WATER
30" 3x(·008")   60" fast or extra-fast sinking braided butt

WET FLY LEADER
36" 5x(·006")   30" 4x(·007")   60" slow or fast sinking braided butt

Selecting the right leader can be very confusing for the novice, as materials are specified in so many different ways. Nylon can be specified by breaking strain, both in pounds and kilos, or by diameter, in inches and millimetres, and sometimes all four measurements are given. I much prefer the old-fashioned X system, which American anglers have always used. It is simple and shows signs of a return to popularity in Britain. I have therefore used the X system when giving specifications for my leaders, but with the diameter in inches in parentheses. Here is a conversion table for those diameters most often used:

8X	·003 inch	·077 mm		4X	·007 inch	·179 mm
7X	·004 inch	·103 mm		3X	·008 inch	·205 mm
6X	·005 inch	·128 mm		2X	·009 inch	·231 mm
5X	·006 inch	·154 mm				

The situation is further complicated by the fact that Drennan Double Strength, which I use because of its wide availability in Britain, does not quite match the table in all sizes so you should go to the nearest diameter. For my fine dry fly leader that means a ·0035 inch point, which is rated at 1½lb breaking strain. Orvis Super Strong, which is also available but more expensive, fits the table and clearly indicates the X rating.

The standard dry-fly leader is the most widely used, but the fine dry-fly leader comes into its own when using very small flies in the low, clear conditions of high summer. If you prefer a slightly shorter leader, the 3X section can be left out. The leader for fast deep water is used for fishing big heavy nymphs on large and powerful rivers. The wet-fly leader is for fishing traditional downstream wet flies in the early season.

Releasing a seventeen-inch Piddle brown, taken in low water using 7x point.

proportion. That means lines no heavier than AFTM4 and light, sensitive rods.

All of the foregoing is about leaders for dry-fly and nymph fishing. For fishing the traditional downstream wet fly, such tapers are unnecessary, as the stream will straighten the leader.

REELS TO MATCH

Finding small reels to match small-stream rods is not always easy, since a number of major reel manufacturers offer nothing at this end of the range.

About twenty-five years ago, Roddy produced a series of fly reels that bore a remarkable resemblance to a series made by a famous English manufacturer, and I bought three of them at fifty shillings each – that's £2.50 in modern money. Two of them were 3 inches in diameter, on which I use No. 5 lines, and one was 2¾ inches, ideal for the No. 4 line. I have been using them ever since and am only now phasing them out, simply because they are beginning to look very battered, although they still function well. Particularly on my 7-foot rod I like a small and very light reel and for several years I have been using the smallest of the Ryobi MG series, which is both small and light. My initial impression of this reel was that it might not stand up to continuous use, but so far it has proved very successful. If you want to spend more for your reels, it is difficult to look beyond the Hardy Flyweight, Featherweight or Marquis, all of which have a world-wide reputation for reliability.

When it comes to finding reels to match your larger rods, there is no problem as virtually all of the manufacturers produce models of 3½ inches diameter and larger.

LANDING NETS

The type of landing net that I prefer and have used for nearly thirty years is simplicity itself and very inexpensive. It comprises an aluminium hoop, a plastic handle and a loop of elasticated cord to go over the shoulder. There are no working parts to jam or wear out, it can never become unclipped and lost, and it is always ready for instant use. The only problem is that such a net is not easy to come by, as I was reminded recently by a reader of my articles who wrote to ask where he could obtain a net of the type that had appeared in so many of my pictures.

Over the years I have acquired three such nets, the first purchased for the princely sum of twenty-five shillings from Molly Sweet's tackle shop in the town of Usk nearly three decades ago. Twenty years on, Charles Inniss at that lovely fishing hostelry the Half Moon at Sheepwash gave me a smaller net from a one-off delivery from a salesman, and that is the net that I now use for most of my river fishing. More recently, I picked up a similar net for five dollars on a visit to the United States. Apart from replacing the netting occasionally, those landing nets will certainly last as long as I need them.

FLY BOXES

Whether you buy your flies or tie your own, they represent a considerable investment and deserve protection in suitable boxes. My own preference is for simple boxes lined with high-density foam rather than anything more complicated and expensive, such as metal clips, magnets or compartments with pop-up lids. The most satisfactory box has proved to be the type with strips of foam with gaps between; these gaps leave space for the hackles of dry

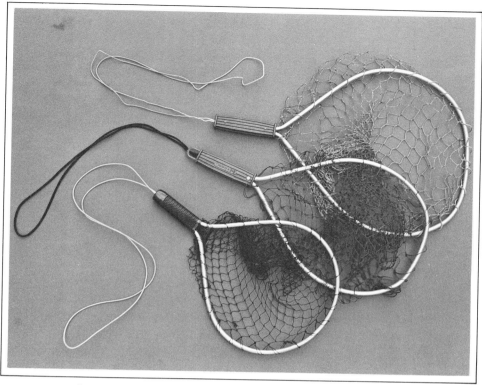

Landing nets (page 42): simple, with no working parts to go wrong.

flies – continuous flat foam results in bent hackles. The only box of this type that I am aware of is the Efgeeco dry-fly and nymph box, which measures 6¼ by 4¼ by 1 inch, and fits easily into the pockets of my waistcoat.

THE ANGLER'S WAISTCOAT

I have never liked using a bag to carry my equipment while actually fishing. The nagging pressure of the shoulder strap is such an irritant that it detracts from the pleasure of fishing and, for me anyway, reduces freedom of movement and efficiency. A commodious bag is essential to carry all the gear that may be called on, but its place is in the boot of the car and it never accompanies me to the river bank. Nothing should hinder the mobility which is such a key factor when seeking wild trout.

However, you will need ready access to numerous items of equipment while fishing. In the early days I managed by stuffing a few items in the pockets of a jacket, but it soon became obvious that something with more carrying capacity was necessary. The answer was a fishing waistcoat and that is what I obtained when they first became available in this country. The only problem was that such waistcoats were fine for fishing with thigh waders, but

THE FLY FISHER'S WAISTCOAT

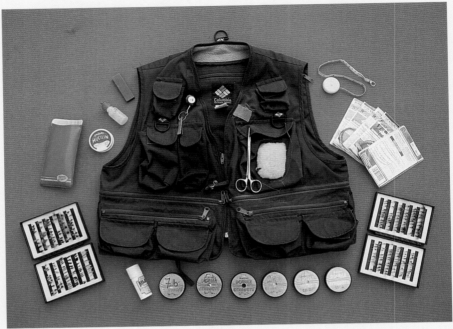

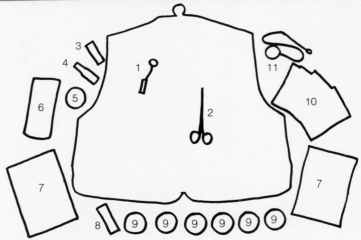

1. Nylon cutter
2. Artery forceps
3. Sharpening stone
4. Fly floatant
5. Line floatant
6. Polarizing sunglasses
7. Fly boxes
8. Insect repellant
9. Nylon for leaders
10. Braided leader butts
11. Tape for measuring trout

Somewhere in those twenty five pockets I had...

a bit too long when used with body waders, and all too often I found that my waistcoat had been trailing in the water and, what was worse, water had seeped into the fly boxes.

As there was no sign of a deep-wading waistcoat appearing on the British market, I sent off to the United States for one of the Columbia range of fishing vests, as they call them, choosing the Henry's Fork II. It has now been in use for five years and really does the job for which I bought it. This waistcoat has twenty-five pockets, according to the manufacturer's catalogue, so there is plenty of space for all of the items that it needs to carry – two or three fly boxes, half a dozen spools of nylon for leader points, a pack of braided leader butts, fly floatant, line grease, artery forceps, nylon clipper, carborundum stone for sharpening hooks, licences and permits, measuring tape and a bit of towelling to wipe the hands.

7
WADING TO SUCCESS

THE USK WAS still running high after the winter rains but it was clear and the late March day held a real promise of spring, with a touch of warmth that by noon had encouraged the dark olives to start emerging. Soon a steady stream of duns was drifting down on the current, just off the willow and alder branches that extend over the river from Prioress Wood, above the town of Usk. The bank dropped steeply to a depth of about two feet and by careful wading it was just possible to work my way out a yard or two into the stream and flick a fly over the trout that were beginning to rise. Several good fish came to my fly and were netted, but I realized that the limits of my thigh waders were preventing me from really getting among the trout. If only I could have waded a foot deeper, it would have been possible to work up the outside of the extending branches and pick off one trout after another. That was a quarter of a century ago and right then I decided that body waders were the answer to that particular situation and a number of others that I had already experienced.

The problem in those days was finding suitable waders at a reasonable price, but eventually I obtained a pair of dark-brown latex stocking-foot waders by mail order – they were Streamrangers imported from the United States. The outfit was completed with a pair of studded wading boots and some old socks to wear between boots and waders. For durability, my choice was a fortunate one, as those latex waders were used for almost twenty years, and even when they were set aside in favour of more state-of-the-art equipment they were still keeping out the water – albeit with the aid of patches.

Naturally, my new wading outfit was put to its first test on the Usk town water and along the edge of Prioress Wood in particular. My anticipation of improved sport was well justified, the long waders making it possible to fish the tree-lined stretches with ease, and without constantly having to pull back just as I was approaching a rising trout.

WADING THE MONNOW

During that same period I often fished a stretch of the Monnow, not far from the Usk. This, however, was a far smaller stream close to the headwaters, but here too the long waders put me in touch with fish that had previously been out of reach. Throughout its half-mile length, this fishery was densely bushed on both banks and the only way to fish was by wading. That was fine on the upper half, where it was easy to fish with thigh waders, but the bottom half, which often held more rising trout, was a different matter. There the stream was backed up by a small weir and the slow water was just too deep for the thigh waders. The arrival of my deep-wading outfit changed all that and I enjoyed many productive sessions, slipping into the stream at the weir and working slowly upstream, casting to trout that previously I could only peer at through the bushes.

For nearly two decades that first deep-wading outfit went with me on many fishing trips and earned me countless trout – but there was one snag. First, the studded wading boots and later, when they wore out, the cleated soles of their replacements were far from ideal for giving a safe grip on the beds of most rivers. Occasionally you fish a stream with an even bed of fine gravel, on which virtually any wader will provide a firm footing, but many streams have rocks and boulders, and then, whether your soles are studded or cleated, you have problems. Whatever the wader advertisements may say, cleats and studs just do not give a satisfactory grip in such conditions.

If I was going to take full advantage of body waders on the more difficult rivers, it was clear that an answer had to be found, for safety as well as comfort. That answer was a wading staff and, although there were several available on the market, I discounted them in favour of a staff of my own making. On all of the staffs then available in the shops the shoulder cord was attached part way down their length. This looks fine until you start fishing, when you find that any loose fly line floating on the surface will often take a turn or two round the top of the staff which protrudes above the link with the cord. The answer was quite simple – the cord would have to be joined to the top, so I made my own staff to a design which I have used ever since.

F E L T   S O L E S

Once I had a staff, I felt confident enough to wade in big powerful rivers, but I was always aware of the shortcomings of my wading boots and their lack of grip on the river bed. Then, on a fishing trip to the United States, I borrowed some felt-soled wading boots and found the sureness of grip an absolute revelation. Unfortunately, I was unable to find any suitable wading boots back home so eventually arranged for some felt-soled boots to be sent across the Atlantic to me.

By then I had finally set aside my old latex waders and gone over to the light-weight nylon waders that have become popular in recent years. My first nylon waders were the original Red Ball, which were being sold off on the Uniroyal stand at the Game Fair. They were certainly light – indeed, so light that it curtailed their durability, but they were soon superseded by a model

MAKING A WADING STAFF

All you need for a simple and efficient wading staff are four ingredients – a suitable piece of wood for the actual staff, a length of cord, a plastic handle from the handle-bar of a bicycle and the rubber butt for the bottom of a walking stick. For the staff itself I go to my local wood and cut some nice straight pieces of hazel or possibly ash, which are then stored for some time to dry and season. Then the wood is cut to a suitable length, which in my case is 4 feet 8 inches (I am 5 feet 8 inches tall), before being rubbed smooth with fine sandpaper and given several coats of varnish.

Next I obtain some braided nylon of about ³⁄₁₆ inch diameter, which is readily available in general stores. The nylon is cut to a length of about 80 inches. One end is threaded through the hole in the plastic handle and then whipped to the top of the staff, before the handle is slid onto the staff and made secure with glue; if the handle is on the loose side, add some extra whipping on the staff to give a firm fit before the final gluing. At the other end of the nylon tie a sliding noose, fusing the end of the nylon protruding from the noose knot with a match. Finally, a rubber butt as used on walking sticks is glued to the bottom of the staff. Some anglers prefer to use lead to sink the bottom end of the staff.

My original latex body waders, perfect for lounging on a muddy Usk bank.

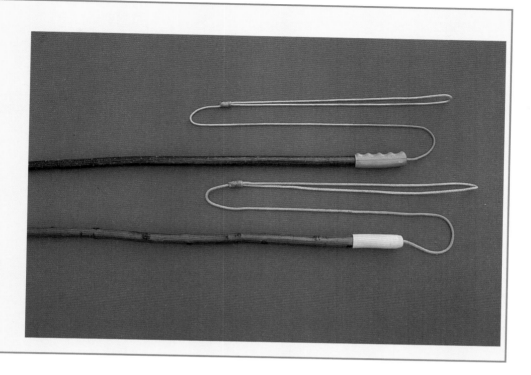

using heavier nylon and I am now using that heavier style.

At present I am also using one-piece felt-soled Snowbee body waders, which offer the convenience that they can be quickly put on and taken off when necessary. Stocking-foot waders and wading boots provide a superbly snug fit, but take some time to put on and are best, therefore, when they are likely to stay on for a lengthy fishing session.

Felt-soled waders have enabled me to discard my wading staff on most rivers, where the bottom is reasonably even and the current not too fierce – another reduction in the equipment that I have to carry. However, the wading staff still comes into its own on big powerful rivers, where the third point of contact with the river bed offers extra security. Today, I use long waders for perhaps half of my trout fishing on rivers and they undoubtedly add significantly to the number of trout I catch. Although I first used body waders on tree-lined stretches of river, there are many other situations in which they more than earn their keep, even on streams where the banks are clear of trees or bushes.

OFF THE SKYLINE

On my favourite stretch of the Suir in Ireland the banks are clear but drop nearly six feet sheer to the surface of the stream, and I know of no way that a small dry fly can be presented delicately to a rising trout from such a high perch. Slip into the river, however, and you have every chance of making the perfect drag-free presentation which is necessary to fool the trout, and you are off the skyline too.

The Piddle in Dorset is a small stream where wading would appear unnecessary, but on some stretches several yards of solid weed stretching out from the bank can make it difficult to get an effective drift over the fish. The only answer is to wade out into the weed, but even on a small stream there are times when the depth is too great for thigh waders.

It is on the really big river that the trout fisher can be at a huge disadvantage without body waders, in the same way that deep wading is virtually essential for salmon fishing on many rivers like the Spey. I recall distant waters such as Henry's Fork on the Snake River in Idaho or the White River in Arkansas where trying to fish with thigh waders would have made the journey virtually pointless, with only the margins at your disposal. Even in my home county of Devon there are medium-sized fisheries on the middle and lower reaches of rivers such as the Exe and Torridge where body waders are essential equipment.

Deep wading offers a further advantage which is not obvious at first. When you are waist-deep in the river with your eyes only a couple of feet from the stream, you suddenly become more aware than ever before of what is drifting down on the current. For the serious fly fisher who likes to match the hatch, this is a real bonus.

There are those who scoff at wading and suggest that it scares the trout and is only a glorified form of paddling. Certainly careless wading is likely to send every fish rushing for cover, but so does careless walking along the bank. Skilled, careful wading, however, is a very different matter and with experience anyone with a reasonable sense of balance can learn to ease his way through the water. With a little care, you will be amazed just how close a feeding trout can be approached. And, if you have doubts about your balance, there is always the wading staff to come to your aid.

The simple fact is that, used in the right way, deep wading is the key to success on many of the rivers that offer the best fishing for wild trout.

PART THREE

8

MATCHING THE HATCH

Few aspects of fly fishing have given rise to more discussion over the years than the relative importance of imitation and presentation. In the early years of this century exact imitation became almost a religion on the chalk streams, but such orthodoxy inevitably leads to reaction and since then we have seen many anglers suggest that presentation is far more important. A few have even suggested that imitation is pointless and that presentation is everything.

All of this is great fun and food for endless discussion and correspondence in angling journals, but at heart it is a sterile argument. Surely logic dictates that the successful angler is the one who has mastered presentation but who can, when necessary, select an effective imitation of the insect being taken by the trout. So let's kill this argument stone dead once and for all and agree to use the best possible suggestion of the natural insect that conditions demand and ensure that our casting and presentation are as good as our natural ability can make them.

Assuming a reasonable level of co-ordination, presenting a fly effectively can be learned either by experience or – a short cut – by expert tuition. Putting together a selection of flies to meet the demands of fishing for wild trout on a variety of waters can be a bit more of a problem. Through the course of a season, the trout in a natural environment will switch from insect to insect, as first one fly and then another increases in numbers, reaches its peak and then declines. Sometimes insects conveniently peak at different times, but there are occasions when several flies are at the peak of their cycles, when the trout may be taking everything that comes their way or selecting one particular species. For success, the angler must have enough knowledge of entomology to know what is going on so that he can react accordingly.

BASIC ENTOMOLOGY

I have no intention of going into entomology in any great depth, as this one aspect of fly fishing has produced countless books in its own right, so I will

FLIES AND THEIR IMITATIONS

NATURAL INSECTS	DRESSINGS	SIZES	STANDARD PATTERNS
Large dark olive (Baetis rhodani)	Page 56	16	Blue Upright, Rough Olive Greenwell, Imperial
Medium olive (Baetis tenax)	Page 58	16, 18	Gold-Ribbed Hare's Ear, Beacon Beige, Dogsbody
Pale watery (Baetis bioculatus)	Page 56	18	Blue Quill, Last Hope
Small spurwing (Centroptilum luteolum)	Page 56	18	Blue Quill, Last Hope
Iron blue (Baetis pumilus)	Page 56	18	Iron Blue
Blue-winged olive (Ephemerella ignita)	Page 83	16	Orange Quill, Blue-Winged Olive, Pheasant Tail (spinner)
Mayfly (Ephemera danica)	Page 72	12	Numerous Mayfly patterns, Grey Wulff, Yellow Humpy
March brown (Rhithrogena haarupi)	Page 56	14	March Brown
Olive upright (Rhithrogena semicolorata)	Page 56	16	Blue Dun, Olive Quill
Black gnat (Bibio johannis)	Page 67	18	Black Gnat
Hawthorn (Bibio marci)	Page 68	16	Hawthorn
Sedges (various)	Page 60	14, 16, 18	Little Red Sedge, G & H Sedge, Walker Sedge, Elk Hair Sedge, Cinnamon Sedge
Beetles (various)	Page 78	16, 18	Coch-y-Bonddhu, Eric's Beetle
Caterpillar (Tortrix viridiana, etc)	Page 112	12, 14	Green Caterpillar
Wood ant (Formica rufa)	Page 80	16	—
Midges (various)	Page 79	20, 22, 24	—

suggest that you obtain a book such as John Goddard's *Waterside Guide*, which should make it possible to identify every insect of importance that you are likely to meet by the waterside. However, there is a relatively short list of insects that are so widespread and numerous that every angler should be able to identify them immediately and have imitations ready for action.

Even the novice should have little difficulty in identifying the flies that emerge early in the season, especially on those rivers that open in March. Then the only fly of consequence is the large dark olive (*Baetis rhodani*), and a rise to a flurry of duns on a chilly day must be one of the most exciting experiences in fly fishing, as suddenly you realize once again that trout will rise up and take that unlikely creation of fur and feather that you have cast on the water. The March brown (*Rhithrogena haarupi*) arrives at the very end of

During a hatch of medium olives it took a size 16 Hackle Adams.

March and in early April, but you have to be lucky to fish a river with a hatch of this splendid great insect – one of the best reasons I know for visiting the Usk in early spring. Another fly of early spring, an improbably early time for a sedge, is the grannom (*Brachycentrus subnubilus*). On some rivers the trout respond well to the grannom, yet on my local River Teign, although it hatches well in April, the trout are not impressed.

In late April and early May there tends to be a natural lull in the hatches and then, around the middle of May, things really get moving, the start of a wonderful period of five or six weeks during which the best hatches and fishing activity of the season will be concentrated. Depending on the rivers that you fish, you can expect to see good hatches of olive uprights (*Rithrogena semicolorata*), pale wateries (*Baetis bioculatus*), small spurwings (*Centroptilum luteolum*), iron blues (*Baetis pumilus*) and medium olives (*Baetis tenax*), emerging over long periods on many days. The black gnat (*Bibio johannis*) will be swarming, especially on the rain-fed rivers, and its cousin the hawthorn (*Bibio marci*) will be blown onto the stream from time to time. The sedges too will have become increasingly numerous, with both daytime and evening activity. Even the blue-winged olives (*Ephemerella ignita*), normally associated with high summer, will be hatching by early June. And, above all, there is the prospect of the mayfly (*Ephemera danica*) carnival. Altogether, this is a period of plenty for the trout and potentially confusing to the angler, but learn to identify what the trout are taking and match it effectively and the results can be dramatic.

TERRESTRIAL TIME

By late June these wonderful daytime hatches will be subsiding and many anglers will be turning to the evening and the hatches of blue-winged olives and sedges that will continue all summer. Fortunately, insect life of another kind is beginning to dominate during the day. Now the aquatic flies no longer hold sway but the population of terrestrial insects explodes in the summer months. Beetles, bugs, ants, caterpillars and various species of Diptera find their way to the surface of the water throughout the day and keep the trout interested at a time when otherwise little would stir. September, the final month on most rivers, sees a return to daytime hatches of a number of upwinged flies, including pale wateries, iron blues and blue-winged olives.

Many of these insects can be matched reasonably successfully with flies from the shelves of tackle shops, but the real essence of wild trout fishing is difficult to capture unless you tie your own. The process of building up a comprehensive knowledge of the natural insects and developing your own range to imitate them is something very special – all part of being in tune with the life of the river and the wild creatures you are trying to catch. In a few cases it is not a matter of preference but necessity, as a number of patterns essential if you are to cope with all eventualities are just not available from the commercial tyer. Try, for example, to get something to cope with the tiny terrestrials of high summer and you are likely to be very disappointed.

Tying your own flies can be wonderfully liberating. When you start, it is inevitable that your first flies are tied in the standard styles with the materials specified, but gradually you gain the confidence to experiment with materials and colours – and, perhaps most important of all, to develop your own styles of dressing the various groups of insects.

HACKLE DUNS

The duns of the upwinged flies, for example, offer endless opportunity for experiment and have inspired many styles of dressing. Many traditional patterns have an opaque upright wing of blackbird or starling, or, more recently, the tips of cock hackle fibres. There have been parachute dressings, upside-down patterns and many more, but my own preference has always been for simple hackled duns, perhaps because they are so easy to tie. Where my own style differs from the standard is in the position of the hackle, which is wound slightly back from the eye, with several turns of body material in front of it. To my eye, this style produces a well proportioned fly and the trout seem to agree. For bodies I have virtually standardized on fine fur from a variety of animals, and now rarely use such materials as peacock quill, feather herl, raffia, silk or floss.

For spinners, the arrival of poly yarn wings changed everything for me. Suddenly spinners could be turned out quickly and the difficult placing of horizontal wings was no longer necessary. All you need is a small clump of the poly yarn, usually in a very pale colour, which is placed horizontally at right angles to the hook shank and tied in, after which both ends of the material are held together above the hook and clipped to ensure wings of even length. Finally, the body material is wound figure-of-eight round the base of the wing to form a neat thorax and the result is a very tidy spinner, which is easily tied, right down to the smallest sizes. A forked tail is a refinement of real value, as it helps the fly to float flat in the surface film where the trout expect to find it. Such a tail is easily achieved by starting with a tiny butt of the body material and then tying in three or four cock hackle fibres to splay out on each side of it.

HOOK CHOICE

Yet another advantage of tying your own flies is the freedom to use hooks of your own choice, and this is particularly so when the practice of catch-and-release necessitates barbless hooks. It makes it possible to select the shank length of your choice, the width of gape, the gauge of the metal – and even to use special hook shapes for imitating such creatures as shrimps.

When I started tying all of my dry flies on barbless hooks a dozen years ago, I first used the Mustad 94845, which is so widely used in the United States, but found eventually that in size 18, on which so many of my flies are tied, the gape is very narrow in proportion to the hook as a whole. Then I was introduced to the Partridge Arrowpoint Barbless (CS20) and have for many years used this hook for virtually all of my dry flies down to 18, the smallest size in the range. For smaller flies I use the Partridge Captain Hamilton Dry Fly (L3A), which goes down to size 22. For wet flies there are plenty of hooks to choose from but I have found the Partridge Sproat Wet Fly (G3A) to meet most of my needs.

In this and the following chapters I give the dressings that I use to imitate or suggest a wide range of insects. However, in the same way as many of these have evolved from the dressings of other anglers, please feel free to adapt them to your own needs. There is nothing sacred in any fly dressing.

THE HACKLE DUNS

The sight of a hatch of duns sailing downstream with their wings erect is one of the most exciting experiences in angling, and every fly box should include a selection of patterns which match the duns of the main ephemeropteran species. Here is my own series of simple and easy-to-tie hackle duns, all with the hackle set slightly back from the head, with some of the body material wound in front. All have dubbed bodies, using fine-textured fur or a substitute.

LARGE DARK OLIVE
HOOK: *16*
TAIL: *Dark blue dun cock hackle fibres*
BODY: *Dark olive fur dubbed on yellow silk, with a few turns of silk exposed at the rear*
HACKLE: *Dark blue dun cock*

MARCH BROWN
HOOK: *14*
TAIL: *Brown cock hackle fibres*
BODY: *Dubbed hare's ear with ribbing of fine gold wire*
HACKLES: *Brown and grizzle cock, one wound through the other*

OLIVE UPRIGHT
HOOK: *16*
TAIL: *Medium blue dun cock hackle fibres*
BODY: *Medium olive fur dubbed on yellow silk, with a few turns of silk exposed at rear*
HACKLE: *Medium blue dun cock*

IRON BLUE
HOOK: *18*
TAIL: *Very dark blue dun cock hackle fibres*
BODY: *Mole's fur dubbed on crimson silk, with a few turns exposed at rear*
HACKLE: *Very dark blue dun cock*

PALE WATERY AND SMALL SPURWING
HOOK: *18, 20*
TAIL: *Pale blue dun cock hackle fibres*
BODY: *Dubbed light olive fur*
HACKLE: *Pale blue dun cock*

BLUE-WINGED OLIVE
See Chapter 13

These are the duns of the species most commonly seen on British rivers, but colours can easily be varied for other species and I have used the same style of dressing to produce imitations of duns on American streams.

SIMPLE EMERGERS

Producing an emerger or floating nymph to imitate the stage when ephemerid nymphs change into duns has been tackled in many ways. As usual, I go for the simplest dressing that is acceptable to the trout and end up

Patterns for the Ephemeroptera

Iron blue (dry)

Large dark olive (dry)

Mayfly nymph

Blue-winged olive (dry),
daytime dressing

Pale watery (dry)

Hackle point emerger

Compara-emerger

Rusty spinner (dry)

Mayfly dun (dry)

Comparadun (BWO dry),
evening dressing

Gold-ribbed hare's ear

Mayfly spinner (dry)

March brown (dry)

with something similar to the duns, but with only vestigial wings of hackle points or deer hair and no hackle. These flies drift down right in the surface film, which is where the trout are expecting to see them, and have often proved effective when duns, riding up on their hackles, have been refused.

Possibly the original emerger was the Gold-Ribbed Hare's Ear, which has worked well for me when medium olives have been hatching.

GOLD-RIBBED HARE'S EAR

HOOK: *14, 16*
TAIL: *Guard hairs from a hare's ear*
BODY: *Dubbed hare's ear with
gold wire rib, with the hair
picked out with a needle at the
front to suggest thorax and legs*

For the smaller emergers, such as pale wateries, iron blues and small spurwings, I use this hackle-point dressing, with the same colour schemes as the duns on page 56.

HOOK: *16, 18*
TAIL: *Cock hackle fibres of
appropriate colour*
BODY: *Dubbed fine fur of
appropriate colour, tied thick for
the front third to form the thorax*
WINGS: *Hackle points of
appropriate colour, about ⅛ inch
long, sloping back over the body*

Wind half of the thorax, then tie in the wings, before completing the thorax, so that the wings slope back from the middle of the thorax.

The American compara-emerger with a short deer-hair wing gives slightly more buoyancy and I often use it for the larger species such as dark olives and blue-winged olives.

HOOK: *14, 16*
TAIL: *Cock hackle fibres split by
a small butt of body material to
produce a forked tail*
BODY: *Dubbed fur of
appropriate colour, thicker at the thorax*
WING: *Short fibres of natural
deer hair sloping back, with some
of the thorax wound in front*

9
TYING WITH DEER HAIR

D EER HAIR IS a wonderful material for the fly tyer and especially for tying dry flies for trout. There is nothing new in that statement, yet in England deer hair remains a relatively underused material, especially for imitative flies, and it is to the American angler that we have to look to see the many advances that the imaginative use of deer hair has brought to the production of floating flies.

The use of hair is probably as old as fly tying itself, but for long it was used mainly in the tying of large lures, whether in early bucktail dressings or the more recent Muddlers. In the last two or three decades, however, deer hair has found increasing favour in the production of duns, spinners, emergers, sedges, beetles and other small imitative dressings. The great advantage that it brings to tying dry flies is the fact that, provided that you select the right variety, deer hair is a buoyant material which offers added floatability.

The key to success is being very selective when buying deer hair, especially as the even tips required for small flies are the exception rather than the rule. Short even hair from the body of the deer is what you are looking for, with the thick butt ends that are of cellular construction and such an aid to buoyancy. The deer hair that I use is mainly from the black-tailed deer and white-tailed deer of America and has been purchased on trips to that country. Good tackle shops in the United States usually carry an excellent range of deer hair, but even there it is necessary to make a personal selection from as wide a range as possible. A piece of deer skin with even-tipped hair is well worth looking for.

I first became aware of the use of hair for dry flies at least a quarter of a century ago when Terry Thomas popularized the Hairwing Sedge and over the years variations on that pattern have caught countless trout for me. The sedge is often thought of as a late-evening fly and dragging a sedge at dusk has often saved an otherwise mediocre evening, but the sedge has produced far more trout for me at other times and fished in other ways. Once early summer arrives, there is usually the odd sedge to be seen throughout the day and it is then that a small Hairwing Sedge can become almost a standard pattern, especially when floated down the quicker broken stretches of a river. The other time when the Sedge really earns its keep is in the early evening, when for an hour or so the hovering sedges are often the only flies to be seen. Then a small hairwing will consistently take a few fish before the more intense action later in the evening when the sherry spinners come back to the river and the blue-winged olives start to emerge.

EVEN TIPS

In the Terry Thomas dressing, the hairwing is tied in and then clipped to the appropriate length, giving a square end. My own preference is to use unclipped deer hair, but that does present the problem of getting a neat finish, without hairs of varying length giving an untidy appearance. Even if you have obtained deer hair with even tips, nature can be improved upon with the use of a tapper or stacker. For years I have used, and indeed still use, the metal cap once used to cover the felt of a Magic Marker. The bunch of hair selected for the wing is pushed into the cap points first, the cap is tapped on the table, and the result should be a hairwing with really even tips. More recently, specially designed hair stackers have become popular in the United States and are now becoming available in this country.

Whether the wing prepared in this way is more effective than the clipped version is questionable, but I find it gives a more pleasing appearance and one of the advantages of tying your own flies is that you can produce patterns that satisfy your own aesthetics – always assuming the trout agree with your taste. Here is the dressing that has proved so successful on countless occasions.

HAIRWING SEDGE
HOOK: *14, 16, 18*
BUTT: *Dubbed orange or green fur*
BODY: *Dubbed hare's ear*
WING: *Natural deer hair*
HACKLE: *Brown cock*

The hairwing sedge can be further simplified by the exclusion of any hackle; the butt ends of the hair wing are left pointing forwards and then clipped to a small, neat Muddler-type head. Sid Neff introduced me to this style of sedge some fifteen years ago and it is now available commercially in the United States under the name of Neff Caddis from Beckies Fishing Creek Outfitters in Pennsylvania.

Sid Neff was also responsible for introducing me to the all-deer-hair beetle, a superb pattern on any tree-lined stream on a summer day. Once again, the natural buoyancy of deer hair means that you can really go for an

Examining a flyboard on the Otter, Devon.

imitation of the natural beetle without the need of a hackle to aid floatability. This pattern is tied with a single clump of deer body hair, which is laid along the shank of the hook and secured with the tying silk wrapped from front to back. The hair protruding to the rear is then pulled forwards to form the back of the beetle and tied in tightly just behind the eye of the hook. All of the hair lying forward of this point will flare out. Clip it to form a fairly bulky head, Muddler-style, except for three or four strands each side, which are left

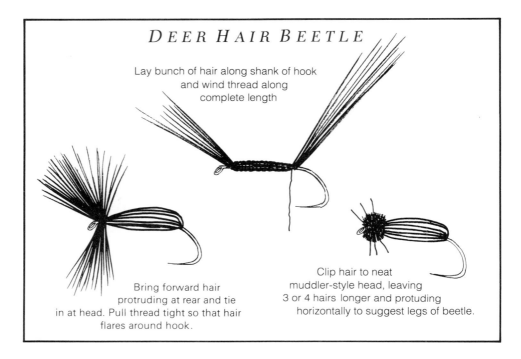

D E E R   H A I R   B E E T L E

Lay bunch of hair along shank of hook and wind thread along complete length

Bring forward hair protruding at rear and tie in at head. Pull thread tight so that hair flares around hook.

Clip hair to neat muddler-style head, leaving 3 or 4 hairs longer and protuding horizontally to suggest legs of beetle.

pointing out sideways to suggest legs. The back is then given several coats of varnish; apart from producing a beetle-like sheen, the varnish also extends the life of the fly, as the rather brittle hair is otherwise easily bitten through by the trout. A strong shiny hair like squirrel tail would be more durable but would not offer the buoyancy of deer hair. Black is easily the most useful colour for deerhair beetles, but I also tie some natural and dyed green.

C O M P A R A D U N S

Deer hair has also become popular for the imitation of the duns of the Ephemeroptera, especially as a result of the introduction of the comparadun by the American angling writers Caucci and Nastasi. In this dressing, flared deer hair replaces the traditional hackle and produces a highly effective and buoyant dun. The deer hair is flared only through 180 degrees, with none protruding below the level of the hook shank, thus allowing the fly to float

Taken on a barbless Deerhair Comparadun, easily removed without handling the fish.

right on the surface film, held there by the deer hair extending horizontally on each side of the fly.

When I took up fly tying, I never really bothered to develop the skill required to tie split wings in the traditional way, as their rather opaque appearance never appealed to me, and virtually all of my duns have been hackle only without a wing. The comparadun offers an ideal alternative with increased floatability and it now enjoys a place in my fly box alongside the hackle patterns that have served me well over the years. I still find it difficult to produce a neat comparadun to imitate the small duns of pale wateries and iron blues, but those that suggest the larger duns such as the large dark olive, olive upright and blue-winged olive have proved very successful.

The deer hair is tied in about one-third of the way back from the eye, with the tips pointing forwards, and the thread pulled tight to make the hair flare through 180 degrees above the hook. The thread is then wrapped in front of the hair to ensure that it is vertical; unless you get things right at this stage, the hair will always tend to lie forward rather than vertical. Next, a small ball of body fur is tied in as a butt, followed by six or eight cock hackle fibres, which are split equally on each side of the fur butt to form a forked tail. The dubbed fur is then wound as a body in the usual way, continuing in front of the hair wing.

A useful variation on the comparadun is the compara-emerger, which comes from the same Caucci and Nastasi stable. The only difference is in the

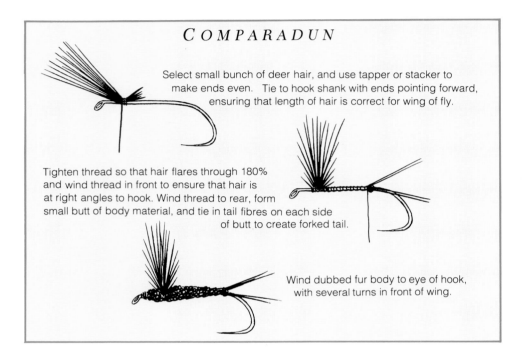

C O M P A R A D U N

Select small bunch of deer hair, and use tapper or stacker to make ends even. Tie to hook shank with ends pointing forward, ensuring that length of hair is correct for wing of fly.

Tighten thread so that hair flares through 180% and wind thread in front to ensure that hair is at right angles to hook. Wind thread to rear, form small butt of body material, and tie in tail fibres on each side of butt to create forked tail.

Wind dubbed fur body to eye of hook, with several turns in front of wing.

deerhair wing, which is much shorter and slopes backwards. This fly is fished right in the surface film when trout are taking ephemeropterans at the point of emergence and at such times can perform far more effectively than an imitation of the dun.

Deer hair can also be used for the wings of spinners, though I now mainly use poly yarn for this purpose because it is so quick and easy to use. And when it comes to the larger dry flies such as the Humpy, the G & H Sedge and the Irresistible, its applications are almost endless.

10
THE ESSENTIAL BLACK GNAT

I SUSPECT THAT most fly fishers keep some sort of record of their fishing trips. In some cases these are full-blown diaries and, in the case of one friend, a detailed chronicle of nearly sixty years of fishing interspersed with beautiful little watercolours. My own records tend to be sketchy, concentrating on notes about those days which offered enough of interest to be worth writing about at a later date.

Whatever form such records take, they can be particularly illuminating when they reveal patterns of fish behaviour, techniques that have brought us success, the times of year that consistently produce the best fishing, and so on. Identifying the patterns that emerge from my own scribbled notes is not always easy, but few things stand out more strongly, year after year, than the reliability of the rises produced by one small insect – the black gnat. Every season, especially on rain-fed rivers, there is a period in late May and early June when huge numbers of this insect emerge and, although the black gnat is a terrestrial species, it has the fortunate habit of swarming over the streams in countless millions.

For the angler on many streams the black gnat's short season offers the first prolonged surface activity of the season. Not only is the natural insect prolific but it is also on the water throughout the day and, most important of all, well liked by the trout. When the black gnat season is at its peak an autopsy will usually reveal the trout's stomach bulging with the natural insect, often to the exclusion of all else.

The name black gnat can cover many small dark insects of the order Diptera, the flat-winged flies, but the species that provides the angler with so many opportunities in the late spring is usually thought to be *Bibio johannis*. It is a small insect with black body and legs and a transparent wing. Through much of the season similar small flies frequently find their way onto the river and, although I have never seen them in the same quantities as during the main hatch, a black gnat imitation is usually worth trying when trout are sipping small insects.

PROLONGED RISES

It is in the period of three or possibly four weeks in late May and early June that I endeavour to be out on my local Devon streams as often as possible to take advantage of the prolonged rises to the black gnat. Yet, while I am enjoying some of the best trout fishing of the season, I am all too often aware that very few anglers bother to make any attempt to imitate the natural. Certainly they will catch some trout by persevering with their Blue Uprights and Greenwell's Glories, but using something that resembles the insect being eaten by the trout is likely to produce more consistent success, especially as the numbers of black gnats peak and the trout become preoccupied with them.

Low water, Upper Teign: black gnat time.

I began to appreciate the importance of the black gnat, especially on rain-fed rivers, a quarter of a century ago. At that time I often fished a short stretch of the Monnow where its upper reaches flow out of the Black Mountains. It was a beautiful little stream, but the fishing, which was rented by the Birmingham Anglers' Association, could only be described as average, except for a short period in late May and early June. In those few short weeks the Monnow became alive with rising trout, but they were far from easy to catch in any numbers. In my innocence and inexperience it took me some time to work out that the cause of all the excitement was the black gnat, and even when the penny dropped it was clear that the flies in my box were not up to the job.

So it was back to the fly-tying bench to produce an imitation of the black gnat that would deliver consistent results. The pattern usually sold in shops, with its upright split wings, bore little resemblance to the natural, a view shared by the trout. The real insect has a slim black body and the pale, almost transparent wing lies flat over the body. Also, it is a small insect, far smaller than the size 16 or even 14 flies usually on sale in tackle shops.

H A C K L E   F I B R E   W I N G

Having consulted the works of Courtney Williams, C. F. Walker, J. W. Dunne and others, I soon realized that over the decades anglers have tackled the imitation of the black gnat in many ways, especially in the treatment of the wing. Hackle points, starling wings, even pike scales were pressed into service, and the Reverend Edward Powell decided to forget the wing altogether and create a hackled pattern called the Baby Sunfly that bore no resemblance to the natural black gnat. Eventually I decided to use a bunch of cock hackle fibres, as suggested by Dunne, but opted for very pale blue dun rather than his mixture of magenta and green, as the light-coloured wing makes the tiny fly more visible, especially on broken water. The resulting simple pattern was as follows:

HOOK: *18*
BODY: *Swan herl, dyed black*
WING: *A bunch of very pale blue
dun cock hackle fibres, sloping
back over the body*
HACKLE: *Black cock*

This fly was an immediate success, and at last my catches began to match the opportunities provided by the frantic surface activity to the black gnat. Only on the really smooth stretches of streams did the sipping trout often refuse my imitation, or take it with a rather unconvincing splash which suggested that they had not been entirely fooled.

Then, in 1968, during a visit to the limestone rivers of Ireland, Sid Neff introduced me to the Jassid and the way he had adapted it to imitate our black gnat. The Jassid had been developed by Vince Marinaro on the limestone rivers of Pennsylvania to imitate the Japanese beetle, with a wing made from the eye feather of the jungle cock lying flat over the body of the fly. Sid's adaptation to match the black gnat replaced the jungle cock feather with a pale blue dun hen neck feather clipped to the shape of the fly's wing.

HOOK: *18*
BODY: *Fine black fur, dubbed*
HACKLE: *Short-fibred black cock,
wound over the body palmer-
style and clipped top and bottom,
so that only the horizontal fibres
remain*
WING: *Small hen neck feather,
very pale blue dun or pale grey,
clipped to the shape of the wing,
laid flat over the body*

The durability of the wing can be increased by a light coating of varnish and a spot of adhesive fixes the wing to the fly body to keep it in position. This fly floats flat in the surface film and has proved an answer to those sipping fish on the flats, which will often ignore a high-riding fly.

POLY WING

Now, more than twenty years later, I am still using what are essentially the same two dressings. However, my original dressing with the hackle fibre wings has changed in two ways. First, for the wing, I now use white or very pale grey poly yarn, which is durable, water-repellent and easy to tie in. The other change is in the use of a body of black fur of very fine texture dubbed onto waxed silk. Although this pattern is very durable, the large number of fish that it catches in the black gnat season inevitably take their toll, so the fact that it is a quick and easy fly to produce really pays off when tying replacements. So the final dressing is as follows:

HOOK: *18*
BODY: *Fine black fur, dubbed*
WING: *White or very pale grey poly yarn, tied sloping back low over the body*
HACKLE: *Black cock*

Although locating rising trout is not always easy, especially on rain-fed rivers, the black gnat season is one time when you can expect to spot rising fish all along the river. Look out especially for the really dense swarms of fly, often over the broken water near the head of a pool. There should be plenty of rising fish in the vicinity and some of the smaller trout may be throwing themselves out of the water to catch the flying insects. All you have to do is present your black gnat imitation to the rising trout in the usual way and you should be in business.

Over the years the black gnat has given me some of my best catches of trout on rivers of many types in many different areas. Wooded stretches of moorland streams like the Teign or the Lyn may be the obvious choice, but I can recall wonderful sport on lowland meadow streams like the Culm in Devon and the Suir in Ireland.

Finally, a word of warning. Black-gnat fishing can be really hectic and an apparently ample stock of flies can easily become depleted. After many years of black-gnat fishing I still get caught out, especially when on a trip away from home and the fly-tying bench. So make sure that by the middle of May your fly box has a really good stock of that wonderful fly, and make the most of some of the season's best sport.

11
THE CHALLENGE
OF THE MAYFLY

I CAME LATE to mayfly fishing, perhaps a dozen years after first casting a fly to a trout, so I had plenty of time to absorb much of the extensive literature on this single insect, before putting theory into practice. Not surprisingly, therefore, I approached my first practical opportunity with a degree of confusion, such was the variety of opinions about mayfly fishing and the extraordinary range of patterns designed to imitate this insect. I had, of course, heard the tag 'duffers' fortnight' used to describe the short mayfly season and, like any novice angler, I was attracted by the thought of easy pickings, with large trout coming freely and frequently to my fly. Yet many writers offered words of warning. In *Fisherman's Fly*, David Jacques suggested that 'fishing the artificial mayfly is not an easy business; on the contrary, it was described by Halford as perhaps the most difficult form of dry-fly fishing, taking one season with another.' And C. F. Walker in *Brown Trout and Dry Fly* sowed a few more doubts, though he eventually came down in favour of mayfly fishing and admitted that he enjoyed it. And early on my appetite had been whetted by the evocative descriptions of mayfly fishing on the Kennet and Coln by Bernard Venables in his *Fisherman's Testament*.

Then there was the wonderful diversity of fly patterns – enough to fill a fly box or two with different imitations of this one insect. Fanwing, straddlebug, fore-and-aft and many other styles had been pressed into service, often resulting in flies that appeared as much like a chaffinch as a mayfly. So what should I use when confronted by a trip to Ireland in 1968, which was planned to coincide with the mayfly hatch on the Suir. By then I had already acquired a taste for hackled dry flies so when I obtained a copy of *Trout Flies for Irish Waters* by Michael Kennedy from the Inland Fisheries Trust I quickly identified the dressing given for the Moseley May as a pattern to my liking.

M O S E L E Y   M A Y
TAIL: *Three brown fibres from a
pheasant's tail feather*

BODY: *Mixture of hare's ear and yellow seal fur, ribbed with gold wire*
HACKLE: *At shoulder only, a long-fibred green-grey olive cock hackle, with a few turns of short-fibred light yellow cock hackle run through it*

I also tied a few variations borrowing the hackles specified for the Gaulden's Favourite – a red cock mixed with a hot orange cock, with a grey mallard dyed greenish-olive in front. Both patterns were well chosen and worked well during my Irish trip, not only on the Suir but also on the Maigue, Camogue and Little Brosna.

The mayfly often brings up the bigger fish, like this Piddle three-pounder.

DEVON MAYFLY

Since those first experiences in Ireland, I have managed a day or two of mayfly fishing in most seasons, sometimes on the chalk streams of Wessex or the limestone streams of the Cotswolds, but more often on my local rivers in Devon. The far south-west is not usually thought of as a stronghold of the mayfly and the streams that rush down from Dartmoor and Exmoor are hardly to the fly's liking. However, the slower streams that meander through the meadows of lowland Devon often enjoy prolific hatches and have given me many great days with the mayfly. Some, like the Culm, really look the part, with many of the characteristics of a chalk or limestone stream, but small streams lying well below the meadows between their deep-cut clay banks, such as the Thrushel, Carey and upper Torridge, can also produce splendid mayfly fishing.

As the years went by my fly box gradually filled with the various styles of mayfly, as I rushed to the fly-tying bench after reading about each new wonder pattern. Then I found myself one beautiful late May day on the Culm in east Devon. Shortly before noon the mayflies started to hatch and continued right through the afternoon, in the steady stream that keeps the trout interested without becoming sated. Right from the beginning they were willing to take my mayfly, a hackle pattern similar to the one I had first used in Ireland. Fish after fish was caught and returned and the flies had to be changed frequently as they became waterlogged. As the day wore on I changed from one style of mayfly to another and all were met with equal enthusiasm by the trout, until I gave up after reaching a total of forty browns by the late afternoon.

STANDARD HOOK

Similar experiences on subsequent days made me begin to think that any fly that looked reasonably like the natural would do, so I turned my attention to evolving a pattern that would be quick and easy to tie, with improved floatation if possible. Starting with the hook, I decided that the size 10 long-shank that was virtually standard for the mayfly was far too heavy, so why not scale down to a size 12 with a standard dry-fly hook? With this size of hook it is possible to produce a fly that is plenty large enough to represent the natural insect and I have stuck with the standard size 12 ever since. Not only does it float better, but a fly of this size offers less resistance when cast than some of the much larger mayfly patterns, and avoids the irritating kinking of the leader produced by large dry flies.

In designing a simple fly I aimed for a straight representation of the colours of the natural – heavily veined wings of grey tinted with yellow green, a creamy-yellow body with brown markings, and very dark tails. For the tail I started with the traditional pheasant tail fibres but more recently I have changed to the dark hairs from a moose, which are stiffer and more durable.

The creamish-yellow body has often been imitated with natural raffia but I always prefer the softer appearance of fur and that is what I use in the appropriate colour, with a ribbing of dark-brown silk. The variety of colour in the wing can be matched with a mixture of cock hackles – slate-grey and yellowish-green for the basic colour, with a well marked grizzle hackle to

Thrushel brownie: one of the magnificent eighty

suggest the veining. So the resulting pattern, which proved to be an immediate success, was as follows:

MAYFLY DUN
HOOK: *12*
TAIL: *Four or five fibres of dark moose hair*
BODY: *Creamish-yellow fur, ribbed with dark-brown silk*
HACKLES: *Slate-grey cock, yellowish-green cock, grizzle cock, wound through each other to mix the colours*

In practice, the number of hackles can be reduced to two, one of greenish-olive and the other grizzle, and the old trick of including a hot-orange hackle in the mix is always worth a try. Yet another variation is the use of a pink body, which I came upon by accident. I was tying up some mayflies and noticed a piece of pink fur which had produced some very effective shrimps. On the spur of the moment I tied several Mayflies with the usual hackles and tail but with a pink body, and a few days later enjoyed a remarkable day on the Thrushel in west Devon when eighty trout were taken on this new pattern. It really does confirm my belief that when the trout are on the mayfly they will take any reasonable suggestion of the natural, so why not stick to a simple hackle pattern that is quick to produce?

THE SPENT GNAT

One of the greatest sights to confront any fly fisher must be a really big fall of mayfly spinners – the spent gnats, as they are known. They fall dying on the water, usually towards evening, with their last quivers sending out concentric rings over the surface, giving the awaiting trout a wonderful opportunity for a feast. The fish know there is no chance of the flies escaping and they can settle down to feeding with the quiet rises that are so exciting for the watching angler. In fact, they sometimes feed so steadily and so long when the fall of spinners is really big that eventually they lose interest. I even recall an occasion on the Evenlode in Oxfordshire when there were so many spent gnats on the water that the normally greedy chub eventually gave up, leaving a river covered with fly but with not a rise to be seen.

My early efforts to suggest the spent fly used grizzle hackle points for the wings and, although the fly looked good enough and caught fish, the wings were not stiff enough and often got caught by the bend of the hook. Using a long-fibred cock hackle, with the fibres in two horizontal bunches at each side, proved much more satisfactory and served me well until I went over to poly-wing spinners and the pattern that I now use.

MAYFLY SPINNER
HOOK: *12*
TAIL: *Four fibres of dark moose hair, split by small butt of body material to form a fork*
BODY: *Rear two-thirds creamy-white fur or synthetic substitute, with black silk rib; front third black fur or synthetic substitute, wound figure-of-eight behind and in front of the wing*
WING: *Very pale grey poly yarn, tied horizontal at right angles to the hook shank*

The wings should be clipped slightly shorter than the natural would suggest, so that they retain enough stiffness to stand away from the body at all times.

AN EFFECTIVE NYMPH

For an effective mayfly nymph we need look no further than Dick Walker's pattern, which I adapt slightly as follows:

MAYFLY NYMPH
HOOK: *8 long-shank*
TAIL: *Five fibres from a cock pheasant tail*
UNDERBODY: *Lead wire*
BODY: *Rear two-thirds creamy-white fur or substitute, with brown silk rib; front third of the same material, wound thickly to form a thorax*
WING CASE: *Cock pheasant tail fibres tied over the back of thorax*
LEGS: *Cock pheasant tail fibres, sloping back at the sides of the fly*

I am sure that anglers who fish more often in mayfly time than I do will tell me that my approach to mayfly patterns, especially the duns, is far too simplistic. Perhaps they are right and more frequent aquaintance would reveal shortcomings in my simple hackle duns, but so far I have had no cause to complain about these patterns and will certainly stick with them until experience suggests a new approach.

12
TERRESTRIAL TIME

*E*ACH SEASON THERE comes a time, probably around late June, when there is a distinct change of emphasis in the feeding habits of the trout, especially wild trout on rain-fed rivers. This change is most evident through the daytime hours when the observant angler will realize that the hatches of upwinged flies which, all being well, have provided splendid fishing for surface-feeding trout through May and June have declined and are now virtually confined to the evening emergences of blue-winged olives.

By now, rivers will be shrinking to summer levels and the combination of bright sunshine and clear water will be making daytime fishing increasingly difficult. Indeed, many fly fishers on rain-fed rivers give up daytime fishing and turn their attention to the evening hatches. The difficulties can at times be so daunting that I can sympathize with their reluctance, as they see it, to face the frustrations of fishing through the heat of the day. All too often even the most careful approach to the water results in small fish rushing up the pool you are about to fish and scaring the better trout you have spotted. And once you are in the water it seems almost impossible to move without creating a wading ripple that puts the fish down.

I have to confess there are times when I ask myself why I persevere, when I could wait until evening and the hectic sport of the blue-winged olive hatch, or the sea-trout fishing once darkness has fallen. The answer, I suppose, is the challenge, for I can think of no branch of fly fishing that presents more problems than tackling wild trout on the quiet stretches of a rain-fed river in the middle of a warm day in July or August. Even if one gets it right, it is unusual to catch the bigger fish or to take a lot of trout.

BEATING THE ODDS

But the fish are feeding and are there to be caught, and when the occasional success comes your way you really feel you have beaten the odds. At the risk of offending devotees of chalk and limestone streams, I must say I have never experienced fishing on the toughest of such rivers that quite compares with the problems posed by the smoother stretches of a rain-fed stream in high summer – problems which sometimes verge on the insurmountable.

So, if you have a taste for masochism – or, to put it more positively, putting your techniques to the severest test – try a few hours fishing around noon on a bushy rain-fed stream during the dog days. It will certainly sharpen your skills and make most other outings with the fly seem easy in comparison, and the chances are you will have the river to yourself. Here is the way I go about it.

The first priority is to find feeding trout, and that is often relatively easy. Walk quietly along a tree-lined stretch of river and there are the trout for all to see, provided you see them before they see you. Most will be close to, or under, overhanging branches, quietly rising to any suitable titbits that come their way. There, immediately, is the key to the change in feeding habits that has taken place. As the availability of aquatic insects has declined, there has been an upsurge in the numbers of terrestrial creatures, and fortunately many of these find their way to the surface of the river, especially where there are plenty of the bankside trees and bushes from which they can fall.

SUMMER LARDER

This summer larder comes in many shapes and sizes, but high on the list come beetles, caterpillars, various Diptera species and wood ants. If I had to pin my faith on imitating one of these terrestrial insects it would be the beetle that would get my vote, but not the traditional hackled patterns like Coch-y-bonddhu or Eric's Beetle. These are fine for more broken stretches, but if there is one thing that has been driven home to me many times when fishing the flatter water it is the need to get the fly right in the surface film, and that usually rules out the full-circle hackle.

On too many occasions I have seen sipping fish put down, or attracted only to turn away at the last moment, by a high-riding dry fly. The beetle that has proved its worth on countless occasions is the all-deer-hair pattern that originated in America. Colour seems to matter very little, as a variety of species of beetle often come the way of trout. I tie mine in black, green and brown, using the method described in Chapter 9.

SINKING BEETLE

When the rivers are at their lowest and clearest, even this pattern can lose its attraction and then I turn to a small sinking beetle, the Black Bug. For some unknown reason, even the most supercilious trout in smooth shallow water is vulnerable to this fly when presented on a long leader with a very fine point.

Though this pattern sinks quickly, it is usually taken with a visible swirl within a second of its hitting the water if it is going to be taken at all. If it does have time to sink before a trout takes, the draw of the leader along the surface is easily seen by the angler in the smooth water.

Sedges, midges and other favorite patterns

Jassid

Deerhair beetle

Black bug

Pink shrimp

Black gnat (dry)

Wood ant

Black midge

Hairwing sedge, hackled (dry)

Hackle midge

Hairwing sedge, no hackle (dry)

BLACK BUG
HOOK: *16 or 18, sometimes 20*
BODY: *A short length of lead wire
whipped to the shank, with
bronze peacock herl wound over*
BACK: *Crow or other black herl,
secured at front and rear*

Another beetle pattern that has served me well is the Jassid, which evolved originally in Pennsylvania, specially for use on its lovely limestone streams. This is a small fly fished flat on the surface, but the jungle cock eye feather used for the wing makes it easy to follow.

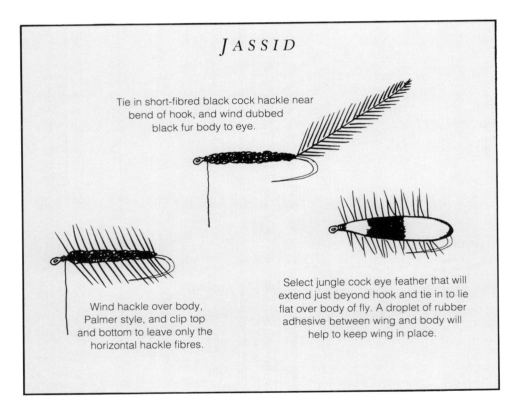

JASSID

Tie in short-fibred black cock hackle near bend of hook, and wind dubbed black fur body to eye.

Wind hackle over body, Palmer style, and clip top and bottom to leave only the horizontal hackle fibres.

Select jungle cock eye feather that will extend just beyond hook and tie in to lie flat over body of fly. A droplet of rubber adhesive between wing and body will help to keep wing in place.

JASSID
HOOK: *18 or 20*
BODY: *Fine black fur, dubbed*
HACKLE: *Black cock, tied in at
the rear and wound over the
body to the head, palmer style,
and clipped top and bottom*

WING: *Jungle cock eye feather*
tied to lie flat over the body; a
drop of glue between the wing
and body helps to keep the wing
in place

Though this pattern started life as a beetle imitation, it works equally well when the trout are taking small flat-winged flies similar to the black gnat. The main black-gnat activity caused by the emergence of *Bibio johannis* may be over by the arrival of summer, but there are several other species that are virtually identical, and these will find their way to the stream from time to time in the summer months. It is always worth trying a Jassid in these conditions.

TINY MIDGES

The huge order of Diptera also includes midges, and, while they may not be as important on rivers as they are on lakes, there are times when a tiny dry midge will make all the difference. These tiny flies need to be tied on really small hooks, but the simple dressings suggested here should not present too many problems. Simplest of all is the Black Midge, with no hackle.

BLACK MIDGE
HOOK: *20 or 22*
BODY: *Fine black fur, dubbed*
WING: *White poly yarn, tied as a*
vertical tuft about one-third back
from the eye

The main purpose of the wing is to make the fly visible and, as no hackle is used, a good floatant must be applied before it is fished, preferably as a thorough application immediately after the fly is tied.

Another simple pattern for those times when the trout are sipping tiny midges is the hackled midge, with a black or grey body and grizzle hackle. As summer progresses, there will also be times when the trout become interested in green aphids, and then this same hackled midge with a bright green body is worth a try.

HACKLED MIDGE
HOOK: *20 or 22*
BODY: *Dubbed fine fur, black*
or grey
HACKLE: *Short-fibred well*
marked grizzle cock

Wherever a river runs through a heavily wooded area, wood ants are likely to find their way onto the river and be taken readily by the trout. If these large brown ants are present, they will be seen crawling along the ground in large numbers carrying woodland debris back to their huge nests. An imitation is easy to tie, with characteristic bulges at front and rear and legs protruding from a narrow waist.

WOOD ANT
HOOK: *16*
BODY: *Dubbed fine brown fur,*
with a distinct ball at front
and rear
LEGS: *Several turns of hackle,*
wound at the waist. Ensure that
the hackle is horizontal, either by
figure-of-eight wrappings or by
clipping it top and bottom.

13
THE BLUE-WINGED OLIVE

'THE BLUE-WINGED olive has rightly been described as one of the most fascinating flies of the dry-fly fisherman's world. Its very name, and that of its imago, the sherry spinner, holds an enchantment which is fully consistent with the stately beauty of the newly hatched insect.' Those words were written by David Jacques in his *Fisherman's Fly* in 1965 and remain as true as ever. Yes, the blue-winged olive, *Ephemerella ignita*, is a wonderful insect, both as a means to the end of catching trout and as a subject for endless argument and discussion.

Few members of the order Ephemeroptera can be more widely distributed and I suspect that I have taken more trout on imitations of its dun or spinner than any other insect. It is also wonderfully reliable, with rarely a day going by during its long season without some hatch of duns or fall of spinners. I can think of many occasions when I have been by the river anticipating a rise of dark olives, mayflies or medium olives and little or nothing has happened, but rarely have I been totally disappointed by the blue-winged olive. And, above all, it is liked by the trout. I cannot recall an occasion when its presence has failed to produce some response from the trout, yet like most anglers I have experienced hatches of other normally desirable insects which have been ignored.

So, whether your fly fishing is on chalk streams, limestone streams or rain-fed rivers, you are putting yourself at a huge disadvantage if you fail to come to grips with the blue-winged olive. It has given me endless hours of pleasure over the years – long summer evenings on my local River Teign, taking my best ever trout from the River Dart high on Dartmoor, frantic sport in an evening downpour on the Derbyshire Wye, autumn hatches in the afternoon on the Wiltshire Avon, duns and spinners filling the air in huge numbers on the Suir in Ireland, and many other vivid memories.

THE ENDLESS CONTROVERSY

As a subject of endless controversy, the blue-winged olive is in a class of its own, and it is the single subject of the colour of the dun's body and how to imitate it that has inspired so many words in books and correspondence columns. Yet there would appear to be nothing very exciting in a description of this insect – indeed, it could almost be described as drab. John Goddard, in his *Waterside Guide* (1988), describes the body of the female dun as being 'bright green-olive, darkening to a rusty-brown-olive as the season progresses'; the male 'varies from orange-brown to olive-brown'. Earlier writers have described the body of the female dun as 'greenish-olive turning to a yellow-brown' (Courtney Williams), 'a strong greenish-olive' (Halford), 'a vivid olive-green to a yellowish-olive' (Harris) and 'greenish-olive' (Taverner). The male's body coloration has been called 'olive' (Courtney Williams), 'reddish under a general colouring of olive' (Taverner) and 'brown orange' (Harris). There is some variation there, but nothing to get too excited about, so it was probably G. E. M. Skues who really set the cat among the pigeons when he discovered that the Orange Quill is an extremely successful pattern when trout are taking the blue-winged olive dun – at least in the evening. Why on earth should such a brightly coloured fly do so well when fish are taking a rather drab insect? That single question is at the heart of so much discussion motivated by the blue-winged olive.

Inevitably, in spite of the stature of Skues, many anglers have come to doubt that the Orange Quill is taken as a dun, but more likely as the sherry spinner with its reddish tinge. David Jacques summed up this argument in *Fisherman's Fly*, observing that the Orange Quill does not resemble the dun but it does resemble the sherry spinner, that during the evening hatch the spinners are also frequently on the water, and that during daytime hatches the spinner is never on the water and at that time the Orange Quill is always refused. He drew the conclusion that the Orange Quill must be taken for the sherry spinner. Yet, in his *Fly Dressing Innovations* (1974), no less a thinker than Richard Walker wrote: 'Colour can sometimes be deceptive. The body of the natural blue-winged olive in its sub-imago stage appears yellowish-green – the colour of a ripe greengage. Attempts to match this colour have failed, because the real colour of the body is orange, overlaid with a slaty-blue integument.' The argument continues!

PRACTICAL PATTERNS

Fascinating though these different opinions may be, at a practical level we each have to identify a series of patterns to deal with the three main situations when the trout are taking blue-winged olives – duns in daytime, duns in the evening and the fall of sherry spinners.

Whether the Orange Quill is taken for a dun or a spinner remains in doubt, but few would quarrel with the fact that the orange fly is a great fish catcher when the blue-winged olive hatches late in a summer evening. The standard Skues dressing for the Orange Quill, given by Courtney Williams in *A Dictionary of Trout Flies*, is as follows:

ORANGE QUILL
HOOK: *16*
TAIL: *Bright red cock hackle fibres*
BODY: *Pale condor quill, stripped and dyed hot orange*
WING: *Pale starling*
HACKLE: *Bright red cock*

My own preference for fur bodies and hackle patterns inevitably led me away from the Orange Quill and a simple hackle Blue-Winged Olive, with an orange body of fur and the hackle set slightly back from the head, has proved its worth in countless hatches.

HACKLE BLUE-WINGED OLIVE
(evening)
HOOK: *16*
TAIL: *Slate-blue cock hackle fibres*
BODY: *Dubbed orange fur, a little wound in front of the hackle*
HACKLE: *Slate-blue cock*

More recently, the comparadun style, described in Chapter 9, has proved equally successful and now occupies an equal place of honour in my fly box. Indeed, the extra buoyancy provided by the deerhair wing gives this fly an edge when floatability is at a premium.

BLUE-WINGED OLIVE COMPARADUN
(evening)
HOOK: *16*
TAIL: *Slate-blue cock hackle fibres, forked around a small butt of body material*
BODY: *Dubbed orange fur, some wound in front of the wing*
WING: *Natural deer hair, flared through 180 degrees*

For all its success in the evening, the orange-bodied fly is a failure when the blue-winged olive hatches during the day, an occurrence that is far more common than most anglers realize. The importance of these daytime hatches, usually in the afternoon, is particularly evident on the rain-fed streams and they are often well established by early June. In most years I take a week's

holiday at the beginning of June, to make the most of the best fishing of the season on the rivers around my home in Devon, and in the last few years the blue-winged olive hatches have on several occasions provided the best surface activity of the day, particularly on the slower lowland rivers such as the Torridge and the tributaries of the Tamar.

THE RIGHT FLY

These hatches can be really prolific and the angler with the right fly can catch a lot of trout in a short time. The right fly is certainly not the Orange Quill. An attempt to match the colours of the hatching duns has proved far more successful and the body shade that I have striven for is the greenish-olive which numerous writers have described as ripe greengage. Fortunately, I have some really fine fur of just the right shade, but more standard colours can be mixed to achieve such a colour if necessary.

HACKLE BLUE-WINGED OLIVE
(daytime)
HOOK: *16*
TAIL: *Slate-blue cock hackle fibres*
BODY: *Greenish-olive fur*
HACKLE: *Slate-blue cock*

LEFT Summer on the Teign: shallow, clear water below Fingle Bridge makes it important to keep low and cast long. Terrestrial patterns are successful during the day, but BWOs take over in the evening.

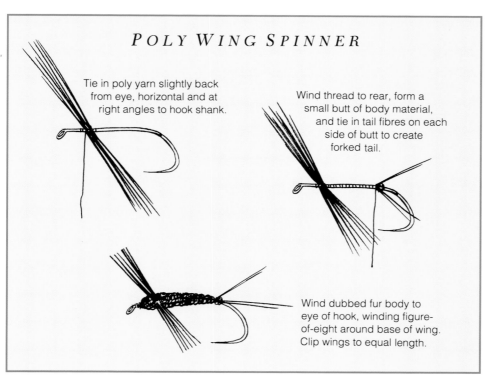

POLY WING SPINNER

Tie in poly yarn slightly back from eye, horizontal and at right angles to hook shank.

Wind thread to rear, form a small butt of body material, and tie in tail fibres on each side of butt to create forked tail.

Wind dubbed fur body to eye of hook, winding figure-of-eight around base of wing. Clip wings to equal length.

As with the evening pattern, the comparadun style can be used by substituting the deerhair wing.

On most summer evenings the sherry spinners begin to swarm over the river quite early and, after laying their eggs, fall dying on the surface, an opportunity for prolonged and confident feeding by the trout. There have been times when the constant sipping rises by large numbers of trout on a smooth stretch of river have appeared almost like rain, a phenomenon I recall vividly from evenings on the Exe below Tiverton when I lived close by.

IN THE SURFACE FILM

My first response to the sherry spinner was the traditional one – the Pheasant Tail. It took fish but never in the quantities promised by the surface activity and I came to the conclusion that with its all-round hackle it was not coming down on the current to the trout in the way that they expected a spinner to appear, right in the surface film. The obvious answer was to clip the hackle top and bottom to give a more spinner-like appearance and that improved things, though the floatation left something to be desired. The next step was tying the fly with the hackle fibres bunched horizontally on each side of the hook, with the body material tied over in figures of eight to give a neat finish.

The result was a sherry spinner with a tail of pale blue dun cock hackle fibres, a body of dubbed reddish brown fur, and a spent pale blue dun cock hackle. I would probably still be using that very successful pattern if it had not been for the arrival of poly yarn in the early 1980s. My first spinners using this material for the wings were an immediate success and I have stayed with them ever since, not only for the sherry spinners but for all of my other spinner requirements. The Rusty Spinner deals with the sherry spinner and others in that colour range, and the body colour can be changed as necessary for other species.

RUSTY SPINNER
HOOK: *16*
TAIL: *Pale blue dun or honey dun cock hackle fibres, forked around a small butt of body material*
BODY: *Reddish-brown fur, tied figure-of-eight round the wing*
WING: *White or very pale grey poly yarn, tied horizontally at right angles to the hook shank*

14
THE CLASSIC PATTERNS

WHATEVER THE PLEASURES of attempting to match the hatching insect with a fly of your own design and making, there will be many occasions when the standard patterns come into their own. If you are not a fly tyer there is no choice unless you can afford to have flies tied to your own specification, but even if you tie your own no fly box should be without a number of the well tried standard patterns that are hard to better.

When it comes to producing a reasonably short list of standard patterns, the choice available can be quite daunting, but if we are concerned primarily with wild trout on rivers large numbers of the more lurid patterns that have been designed for lakes and reservoirs can be ruled out. What we are looking for is a range of flies that includes a few fairly close imitations of those insects that are sufficiently numerous for the trout to take them exclusively, plus some well tried general patterns that suggest whole families of insects.

As I live in Devon, where better to start than with the flies which originated in the county? In fact, it is doubtful if any county has contributed more patterns that have acquired national and even international recognition. The fact that Devon flies are normally hackle patterns means that they can be tied as dry flies or wet flies, by using either cock or hen hackles. I tie the wet patterns on size 12 and 14 hooks, and the dries mainly on 16s, with some 14s and 18s.

Perhaps best known of all Devon flies is the Blue Upright, designed by the prolific R. S. Austin of Tiverton. We are told that it was designed to suggest the willow fly, a small member of the stonefly family, but I have found it particularly useful when the trout are feeding on large dark olives. Whether cast as a dry fly to a rising trout or swung across the stream as one of a team of wet flies, this is a great and versatile pattern.

BLUE UPRIGHT
TAIL: *Slate-blue cock*
BODY: *Stripped herl from a peacock eye feather*
HACKLE: *Slate-blue cock for the dry fly, hen for the wet fly*

R. S. Austin was also the creator of the Tup's Indispensable, a useful pattern in the smaller sizes for imitating pale wateries and small spurwings, as well as serving as a general fly on any type of water. The original dressing specified wool from the underside of a ram for the thorax but I am happy to use fine fur in a dull pink. Alternatively, you can mix fur of several colours in a blender – Dave Collyer suggests sandy coloured fur from a hare, some dark fur from a hare's ear and a little scarlet mohair.

TUP'S INDISPENSABLE
TAIL: *Blue dun or honey dun cock*
BODY: *Rear third yellow floss or*
silk; front two-thirds dull pink fur
HACKLE: *Blue dun or honey dun*
cock for the dry fly, hen for
the wet fly

Wet or dry, there can be few better flies for all-round fishing than the Pheasant Tail, described by Courtney Williams as 'the most useful all-purpose fly extant'. Before changing to poly-wing spinners, I often used a Pheasant Tail in a fall of sherry spinners and took many trout on it.

PHEASANT TAIL
TAIL: *Honey dun cock*
BODY: *Herl from a cock pheasant*
tail feather, ribbed with fine oval
gold wire
HACKLE: *Honey dun cock for the*
dry fly, hen for the wet fly

Two other Devon patterns which are less widely known but equally effective are the Half Stone and Infallible. The Half Stone is another good fly for when olives are emerging, and the Infallible dressing is essentially that of the standard iron blue imitation.

HALF STONE
TAIL: *Blue dun cock*
BODY: *Rear half yellow or*
primrose floss or silk; front half
dubbed mole's fur
HACKLE: *Blue dun cock for the*
dry fly, hen for the wet fly

INFALLIBLE
TAIL: *Dark blue dun cock*
BODY: *Mole's fur dubbed on*
crimson silk, with some of the silk
showing at the rear
HACKLE: *Dark blue dun cock for*
the dry fly, hen for the wet fly

Heaven forbid that I should ever be restricted to a single dry fly but, if I were, that wonderful American standard pattern, the Adams, would probably

The standard patterns

Blue upright (wet)

Tup's indispensable (wet)

Pheasant tail (wet)

Half stone (wet)

Infallible (wet)

Adams (dry)

Coch-y-bonddhu (dry)

Partridge & orange (wet)

Grey duster (dry)

Black & peacock spider (wet)

Soldier palmer (wet)

Yellow humpy (dry)

Hare's ear nymph

Montana nymph

be chosen. With its medium tone, not too dark and not too light, and its colour broken up by the grizzle hackle, it suggests many insects in general and none in particular, though I have found it very successful when medium olives are hatching. This same hackle combination is used in the Beacon Beige, Super Grizzly and Grey Fox Variant. The original dressing has grizzle hackle-point wings, but I often leave these out and the resulting hackle pattern appears to be equally successful.

ADAMS
HOOK: *14, 16, 18*
TAIL: *Mixed grizzle and brown cock*
BODY: *Natural grey muskrat for*
the original dressing; I often use
grey rabbit, which is more
readily available
WING: *Grizzle cock hackle points*
HACKLES: *Grizzle and brown*
cock, one wound through
the other

The Grey Duster serves two functions – it is a great fish catcher and one of the easiest dry flies to tie. In really small sizes, it also serves well when trout are taking adult midges.

GREY DUSTER
HOOK: *14, 16, 18 (plus 20 and 22*
for midges)
TAIL: *None*
BODY: *Rabbit fur*
HACKLE: *Badger cock*

There are times when a really buoyant fly is required and then the Humpy comes into its own, which is hardly surprising as it was created for the big streams in the mountains of the western United States. It is also useful at times when the trout are taking the mayfly.

YELLOW HUMPY
HOOK: *12, 14, 16*
TAIL: *Moose hair, about six fibres*
UNDERBODY: *Pale yellow floss or fur*
BACK: *Natural deer hair*
WING: *Natural deer hair, upright*
HACKLES: *Brown and grizzle*
cock, one wound through
the other

Although my preference in beetle patterns is for the all-deerhair dressing, the traditional fly is the Coch-y-bonddhu, which has a great reputation on moorland streams.

COCH-Y-BONDDHU
HOOK: *14, 16*
BUTT: *Flat gold tinsel*
BODY: *Bronze peacock herl, fairly bulky*
HACKLE: *Brown cock with black centre. If not available, use two hackles, black and brown, one wound through the other*

The classic Devon flies tied with soft hackles cover many of my needs for wet-fly fishing, but there are several other patterns that I would not be without. Speckled brown partridge feathers form the basis of a wonderful series of hackle patterns, the Partridge and Orange probably going into any list of all-time favourites. The orange body can be replaced with yellow or green fur to advantage, and a hare's ear body produces the standard wet March Brown. With a flat silver tinsel body, ribbed with oval silver tinsel, it becomes the Silver March Brown, a first-class point fly for the downstream wet fly method.

PARTRIDGE AND ORANGE
HOOK: *12, 14, 16*
TAIL: *None*
BODY: *Orange fur ribbed with oval gold tinsel*
HACKLE: *Speckled brown partridge*

There are times when a black fly seems to be the only thing that the trout want and then I use Tom Ivens's wonderfully simple reservoir pattern, the Black and Peacock Spider.

BLACK AND PEACOCK SPIDER
HOOK: *12, 14, 16*
BODY: *Bronze peacock herl*
HACKLE: *Black*

On the moors of the south-west, tradition has it that when the rivers are peat-stained there is nothing like a Soldier Palmer. Whether or not that is the case, I like to have this fly on the dropper when fishing the moorland streams

The object of the whole elaborate exercise.

and at times I have found that it works even better if a grizzle hackle is used in place of the brown.

SOLDIER PALMER

HOOK: *12, 14, 16*
BODY: *Scarlet seal fur, ribbed first with short-fibred brown cock hackle and then with fine gold wire to lock in the hackle*
HACKLE: *Brown cock, longer in fibre than the body hackle*

When it comes to nymphs on the stream, it is often difficult to look beyond Frank Sawyer's classic Pheasant Tail Nymph, the dressing for which has been given in countless books since it first appeared in Sawyer's *Nymphs and the Trout*, but I often use a Hare's Ear Nymph as an alternative.

HARE'S EAR NYMPH
HOOK: *14, 16, plus 10 and 12*
long-shank on big streams
TAIL: *Four fibres of cock*
pheasant tail
BODY: *Hare's ear with gold wire rib*
THORAX: *Hare's ear, thicker than*
the body, with wing case of crow
or heron herl
LEGS: *Brown speckled partridge*

For nymph fishing on big fast streams, I use the Hare's Ear Nymph in large sizes, or the Montana Nymph, which was created to suggest the big stoneflies of Rocky Mountain rivers. Both should have variable amounts of weight to suit the conditions.

MONTANA NYMPH
HOOK: *4 or 12 extra-long shank,*
such as Partridge CS17
TAIL: *Four fibres of crow or*
heron primary, tied forked
BODY: *Black chenille*
THORAX: *Yellow chenille*
HACKLE: *Short-fibred black cock*
wound palmer-style over the
thorax only
WING CASE: *Two strands of black*
chenille, over the back of
the thorax

Such a selection of standard patterns should get you started on most waters, but always be ready to seek expert advice when away from home and buy or tie what the locals recommend.

PART FOUR

TRAVELLING FOR TROUT

15
IN SEARCH OF
WILD TROUT

ALTHOUGH I AM fortunate enough to live in one of the most beautiful parts of Britain, the Dartmoor National Park, with a dozen trout streams a short drive from home, I can never resist the opportunity to travel in search of trout, whether in another part of these islands, another country or another continent. The thought of casting a fly on a new stream, be it in Devon or Montana, always gives rise to excited anticipation – an anticipation that never palls as the years go by. Even though I enjoy fishing for other species, it is only the prospect of a trip in search of trout, and especially wild trout, that really gets the adrenalin flowing.

It is, of course, perfectly possible to enjoy a lifetime of trout fishing on just a few local rivers and in different circumstances I might have done just that. When my interest in river trout fishing began to develop, my home was in Gloucestershire on the edge of the Cotswolds, an area of delightful limestone trout streams, but for a young fly fisher of limited means those closely preserved streams might have been on another planet. So my attention turned west to the club waters on the rivers of the Welsh Marches and those early trips of 40 miles to the Usk and Monnow and Wye have in the past three decades increased to 400 and occasionally 4,000 miles. I cannot help thinking that those early financial constraints were a blessing in disguise and without them I might not have enjoyed more than thirty years of trout fishing in many varied and beautiful places.

THE IDEAL FISH

The trout, and especially the wild trout, is just about the ideal fish for the angler who likes to travel in pursuit of his fishing. Indeed, I would suggest that no other fish offers quite the same rewards to the exploring fly fisher.

First of all, the trout has the great merit of being present in the river throughout the year, so you do not have to worry about timing your visit to coincide with a run of migratory fish. I never quite know whether to sympathize with my friends who travel long distances to fish for salmon or to admire their gambling instinct. Unless you are fortunate enough to have the funds to choose a famous fishery, the chances are that only a small percentage of trips will coincide with a run of salmon, and even the most expensive salmon waters can let you down. When the instincts were handed out, they definitely failed to send the gambling instinct my way – I cannot even be bothered to participate in a draw for the Grand National – so fishing for salmon is strictly a day-trip activity for me.

One of the great problems that faces any newcomer to a fishery is that of locating the fish. Salmon and sea trout are often reluctant to show themselves, even when present in good numbers, and other species in fresh and salt water can be very difficult to locate without the services of a guide. The

Drifting for trout: Upper Lough, Cummeenduff Glen.

angler who fishes for trout with a fly, however, has the great advantage that a trout shows itself whenever it takes an insect at or near the surface. The result is that even on a fishery that you have never seen before you can have every expectation of finding fish quickly and making a good catch on your first visit. Some of the best days that I have ever experienced have been on my first visits to a wide variety of rivers.

If you are rich enough to employ a guide or a gillie whenever you take a fishing trip, the problem of finding fish can be solved, but at the same time you risk losing some of the deepest pleasures that fishing can offer. I have, very occasionally, enjoyed the services of a guide but have always experi-

RIGHT Sid Neff fishes Nelson's Spring Creek, beneath the snow-flecked peaks of the Absaroka Range, Montana. That day we caught and released many rainbows and cutthroats.

BELOW Fishing the dry fly among the boulders of the East Lyn near Rockford.

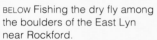

enced a sense that something was missing – the challenge of spotting a rising fish and selecting the right fly. In its place I have the irritation of having to work to someone else's timetable and move on just when I am beginning to enjoy myself – in fact, the overall loss of freedom that is such an important part of a fishing trip.

BEAUTIFUL PLACES

The trout, perhaps above all fish, is widely distributed in some of the most beautiful parts of the world, and every trout fishing trip that I have ever enjoyed I would have been as happy to make for the scenery alone, whether in my own county or much farther afield. Memories of the places trout fishing has taken me to are as treasured as the actual catching of trout. Exploring a tiny boulder-strewn stream tumbling down from the heights of Dartmoor, casting over a crystal-clear spring creek with the snow-clad Rockies as a backdrop, climbing to a mountain lough full of small trout in Ireland or creeping along the banks of a chalk stream in Wessex – all have been rich experiences which I hope to emulate on new waters in the years ahead.

But perhaps the great appeal of the trout for the exploring angler is that some of the very best trout fishing in the world is available to all. Even if you travel to the end of the earth, good salmon fishing can cost you an arm and a leg, but some of the finest trout fishing anywhere can be obtained for the cost of a licence. In fact, virtually all of the fisheries described in the following chapters could be fished by anyone and most still can – some by buying a licence or a permit, others by staying at a hotel or in self-catering accom- modation, and a very few are entirely free of any charge.

If you do decide to travel widely for your trout, you will be faced with one of the most fascinating challenges of trout fishing – mastering the variety of techniques necessary to cope with varying conditions. I recall on one day fishing the smooth currents of the Firehole River in the Yellowstone National Park with small duns and then, the following day, bouncing a huge weighted stonefly nymph in the deep pockets of the big, fast-flowing Madison. Quite often, near my Devon home, I will fish the rough water with a high-riding dry fly in the morning and turn to trout that are sipping tiny spinners on the smoothest pools in the late evening.

ADVANCE PLANNING

The real key to success on any fishing trip is advance planning and this is particularly so the farther you travel from home. The satisfaction that you get out of any expedition will be in direct proportion to the effort that you put in at the planning stage. Far from being a chore, however, time spent on preparation and planning should be a pleasure in its own right. For a new water far from home, this is the time to study maps and fishing guides, dig out relevant articles in back issues of magazines, write to any friends or contacts who can offer local knowledge – in fact, do everything possible to shorten the odds when you actually arrive at a new and strange fishery.

My most recent long-range fishing trip before writing these words was to the White River in Arkansas, USA. Although this was only a brief visit of four days tagged onto the end of a week-long business tour, I spent many enjoyable hours gathering information and planning well in advance of departure – probably more than I did for the business element, I suspect. On arrival at my destination, I resisted the temptation to start fishing right away and devoted the day to gleaning the latest information from local contacts that I had lined up in advance, and then taking a look at all the likely spots they had pointed me towards. My forbearance was more than rewarded over the next three days.

16
THE SUIR

'*I* CAN IMAGINE that in May and June it might be the finest dry-fly fishing in the United Kingdom.' I first read those words which ended the last chapter of Sir Edward Grey's classic, *Fly Fishing*, more than a quarter of a century ago and, although the author revealed that the river in question was in Ireland, I was unable to find any reference to its name. Then, a few years later in 1967, when reading Howard Marshall's newly published *Reflections on a River*, I learned that Grey had been writing about the Suir, a limestone stream that rises in the Devil's Bit Mountain and flows much of its course through Tipperary before becoming tidal at Carrick-on-Suir and flowing past Waterford to the sea.

Tipperary road sign: the right sense of priority.

At that time I was planning a trip to Ireland to sample the dry-fly fishing on its limestone rivers. Although I had by then fished on a number of first-class rain-fed rivers like the Usk, my opportunities to sample dry-fly fishing on a classic chalk or limestone stream had been confined to one day on the Test at Whitchurch. With little chance of extending that experience in England, I had decided that Ireland offered the best opportunity and the words of Sir Edward Grey convinced me that the Suir should be the first stop. Even though his words had been published in 1899, surely something was left to enjoy in a fishing trip that I planned for the spring of 1968. As it turned out, I enjoyed five days of the finest dry-fly fishing that I had experienced at that time, and rarely have I matched it since. I had selected the lovely stretch of the Suir downstream of Holycross Abbey which is controlled by the Thurles, Holycross and Ballycamas Angling Association, mainly on the advice of Des Brennan, who was then Organizing Controller at the Inland Fisheries Trust.

My arrival in Tipperary was late on Saturday. I checked in at the Hayes Hotel in Thurles, where I bought my permit for the next few days' fishing. Next morning, I arrived at Ballycamas at ten o'clock to find a most beautiful stretch of river. Having spent many hours viewing the chalk streams of southern England from a multitude of road bridges, I found it hard to believe that here I had the run of miles of superb dry-fly water without a 'Keep Off' sign in sight.

TWO QUICK FISH

I quickly donned my waders and started off upstream. At the first fast run I came to, a few fish were rising and, although there was little fly about at this stage, I tied on a size 16 Blue Dun and gave them a try. I missed the first two rises but then caught two quick fish – both eleven inches.

About half a mile upstream I came to the mouth of a tributary, the Clodiagh, and from there upstream stretched the most delightful piece of water, very reminiscent of the Kennet (to which the Suir is often likened) but with rather more broken water. A few medium olives were hatching and the odd fish rising, so I slipped into the water and started covering these fish with a size 16 Gold-ribbed Hare's Ear. I had missed several fish and landed one when I realized that the hatch was quickly increasing and that the dominant fly was now the iron blue, and in a matter of minutes I was in the midst of a huge hatch. By now, it seemed that every fish in the river was rising, with at least half a dozen of them within easy casting range, so I changed to an iron blue imitation.

IRON BLUES

The following two hours, in which the iron blues kept emerging in countless thousands, produced the type of dry-fly fishing which we all dream about but seldom experience. The fish rose steadily and, provided that they could be covered without drag, took readily, but these were wild trout and many came adrift as they fought for their freedom. Around two o'clock, the hatch petered out, but by then I had netted eight superbly conditioned trout and was ready for a rest.

OPPOSITE Fly change on the Suir.

When I returned to the river at five o'clock a few spinners had started to come onto the water, but perhaps as a result of the heavy feeding earlier in the day there was little sign of rising fish until I came to a small pool where a sidestream joined the main river, and there several trout were rising steadily. On the assumption that these fish must be taking spinners, I tied on a Red Spinner and four fish quickly came to the fly, three of which were safely netted. Those were the last rising fish I found on my first day, but the total for the day was twelve fish up to a pound and a quarter.

THE AMERICAN ANGLER

As I wandered back to the car I saw striding towards me another angler, who, like me, was clad in full-length body waders. Several times during the day other fishermen had told me of an American who came down from Dublin each weekend and regularly took between a dozen and twenty fish a day. Another visiting Englishman had told me how an American had, on the previous day, taken thirteen fish from one spot while standing waist-deep in the middle of the river. From his general appearance (felt-soled body waders, fishing vest – waistcoat to us – and tennis-racket-type landing net), the subject of these reports was approaching me now. He had heard that I had had a good start to my holiday and stopped to have a chat about the day's sport, a chat which ended some five hours later when the local bar closed at 11 p.m. We found that we had much in common (even our profession, graphic design) and he invited me to join him the following morning – little realizing that it would be the first of many fishing days that we would enjoy together in the next twenty years or more, on both sides of the Atlantic.

At ten the next morning I joined my new friend, Sid Neff, at Twoford Bridge, where he always camped in his Land Rover, and we decided to fish the same stretch as the day before. Today, however, the wind had got up and was blowing strongly downstream, making casting rather difficult. The hatch of iron blues and the rise of fish was as good as ever, but the wind made a perfect presentation almost impossible – and Suir fish are very demanding in this respect. However, in the odd lull it was possible to put the occasional fly in the right place and I finished up with five fish to a pound.

COCHRANE'S FLAT

The next morning we moved upstream, above Twoford Bridge, so that I could see some new water. The morning was quiet and we spent most of it walking along the river, until around noon we arrived at a long smooth stretch known as Cochrane's Flat. Our arrival coincided with the beginning of the hatch, which, instead of being predominantly iron blue, was today fifty per cent little sky blue (*Centroptilum luteolum*), more often known as the small spurwing in England. I stuck with my iron blue and Sid tried an imitation of the little sky blue. During the next hour or so we had seven fish each and later, when passing the same stretch on the way back to the car, I picked up my best fish of the day, a trout of one pound six ounces. Although the main rise was over, this fish was rising steadily all on its own, about three inches from the bank, and took my first cast with a Pheasant Tail tied spent.

On my last two days on the Suir the iron blue was less dominant, though still important. The first of the mayfly were now appearing and in one hectic spell I had six trout up to two pounds on this fly in half an hour, all on a standard Irish pattern, the Moseley May. The grey flag sedge (*Hydropsyche* spp), which is so important on Irish rivers, was always present and an imitation was usually effective except in the hatches of iron blue. There was also a fair amount of Welshman's Button (*Sericostoma personatum*) and the last few hawthorns, which, I was told, had produced good rises in the previous week.

I visited the Suir briefly two years later in the July of 1970 and enjoyed two splendid evenings with the blue-winged olive and sedge, but soon after disquieting reports about the river began to emerge – of pollution of various kinds which resulted in fish kills over extensive lengths of river. These attacks of pollution continued off and on through the seventies and eighties, with intervals when the river recovered and, thanks to its basic fertility, the trout quickly re-established themselves. All too often, unfortunately, there were further outbreaks of pollution before the trout could get back to the size for which the Suir was famous.

RETURN VISIT

The Suir, however, is a river that was bound to pull me back to its banks sooner or later and reports of recovery encouraged me to arrange a return visit in June 1990. With three days to spare, I decided to concentrate my efforts on the stretch of river that I knew from the past, the waters of the Thurles, Holycross and Ballycamas Angling Association. This time I stayed at Ardmayle House, a farm just downstream of the association water, which also has its own stretch of the river.

Even before I started fishing, I was reassured by the fact that the Suir valley had changed little in twenty years, unlike some parts of Ireland where the unplanned growth of bungalows has spoiled once beautiful countryside. The only noticeable change was at Holycross, where the riverside abbey that I had known as a ruin was now restored to its former glory. The river appeared clean, though with the growth of flannel weed on the bottom that is now so widespread on many rivers, but the most encouraging sight was the still-prolific fly hatches and the fact that even at the quietest time of day there was usually the odd rising trout to be seen. An afternoon walk along the river at Ballycamas on the day of my arrival revealed plenty of medium olives and little sky blues, and during an evening session on the farm water I saw plenty

LEFT Twoford Bridge on the Suir: typical of the many beautiful bridges on this river.

BELOW Medium olives were emerging and this Suir brownie took a hackled Gold-ribbed Hare's Ear.

of sedges and blue-winged olives, both duns and spinners. On that first evening the nine trout that I caught were of modest size with nothing over ten inches, but their condition was a revelation. All were deep, fat fish which clearly had access to ample food, and splendidly coloured with yellow bellies and large spots, many of them a bright red.

Next morning I purchased my fishing permit from O'Gorman's Bar at Bohernacrusha and drove down to Ballycamas, parking in the riverside meadow on the right bank. For about a quarter of a mile upstream the river is deep and slow, more suited to fishing the mayfly or a late evening sedge, so I walked up river to where the stream became quicker and shallower. Already the medium olives and little sky blues were hatching and a few trout were rising quietly along the far bank, so I slid down the high, steep bank into nearly three feet of water, easily waded in my body-length waders. If ever a river was designed for deep wading, it is the Suir. Some of the most productive stretches have banks that are six feet high, from which presenting a fly quietly and without drag is almost impossible, apart from the problems of standing out starkly against the skyline. Wading both avoids presenting such a fish-scaring silhouette and makes it possible to cast from a position most likely to ensure a drag-free drift of your dry fly.

ORIGINAL EMERGER

The little sky blue imitation that I tried first produced nothing, even though I covered several steadily rising trout, and a change to a medium olive only took one fish. Perhaps they are still taking the emerging insect, I thought, so on went a size 14 Gold-Ribbed Hare's Ear, perhaps the original imitation of an emerging medium olive. Four trout to twelve inches came quickly with hardly any need to move my position, and then two more as I worked upstream to the mouth of the Clodiagh, a tributary that comes in from the west. All of these trout fought powerfully and jumped frequently, with many fish coming adrift.

By noon I had fished for nearly two hours and took a break until mid-afternoon, when I fished up the same stretch once more. Those medium olives were still hatching steadily and I quickly took a trout on a size 16 hackled Gold-Ribbed Hare's Ear, but the bright light and downstream wind were making things increasingly difficult. In one pool alone I put down six steadily rising trout with what appeared to be perfect presentations. Perhaps the force required to push the fly into the downstream wind and the need to use a slightly heavier leader point than would have been possible on a windless day were enough to warn the trout that all was not well. However, I suspect that even in perfect casting conditions those supercilious fish would have rejected my best efforts.

After dinner, I was back on the river by half past eight, to find that already some sedges were fluttering over the surface. Four modest trout came quickly on a hairwinged sedge, size 16. Then it was the turn of the sherry spinner, which descended on the river in huge numbers, and six more trout were taken on a poly-winged imitation. Finally, a superb hatch of blue-winged olives continued right until darkness and, when I walked back to the car at eleven o'clock, sixteen trout up to about a pound had been caught and released. When the blue-winged olives started hatching the trout were at first difficult, but as the light died they became more confident and eventually virtually every presentation of my orange-bodied Comparadun produced a take, though many fish were lost, especially as they leapt from the river with tails clattering. Although I fished a skated sedge for a few minutes at the end, the result was only two explosive rises and nothing hooked.

F I N A L   D A Y

The next day was very similar, with the evening hatch of blue-winged olives and the rise of trout even more prolific, but on a clear, cool evening the fish were never easy to fool and I had to work hard for my nine trout to thirteen inches. I was in contact briefly with a very good fish, which may well have been a two-pounder, but we parted company on its first shattering jump. As darkness fell, both the sky and the surface of the river were still full of blue-winged olive duns, but the trout had had enough and had stopped rising.

A week later, on the way back from Kerry, I snatched another day on the Suir and fished the same stretch. The morning hatch was rather sparse but trout were rising and I took seven on the hackled Gold-Ribbed Hare's Ear. I also found a good fish rising in the same spot where I had lost the big one a week earlier and again it sucked in my fly without hesitation – and again we parted company, this time on the second jump. In the afternoon, I fished the two miles from Ballycamas up to Twoford Bridge and took eight more trout to twelve inches on the same hackled Gold-Ribbed Hare's Ear.

By evening, the weather had become unsettled with some very heavy showers moving in from the west, but I decided to try once more after dinner as I was returning to England the next day. It was still dry when I reached the river and several fish were taking the sherry spinners, including the big fish of previous aquaintance. Once more it took the first presentation and this time all started well as we were still in contact after two jumps and a searing run, but a third jump was enough to throw the fly, by which time I had seen enough to be sure it really would have gone two pounds. Unfortunately, it was very clear that that trout was not for me.

Having taken three fish, I realized that the rise had slowed and I walked downstream to be nearer the car in case the big black clouds that were gathering produced rain. When the rain did come, it coincided with a hatch of blue-winged olives and a frantic rise, but although I covered fish after fish for half an hour I never had an offer, even though I tried both orange-bodied

When the fish are small and lightly hooked try to shake them off while they are still in the water.

and more natural-coloured imitations. Perhaps the heavy rain was drowning the fly, but the rain-lashed surface made it impossible to see what was going on. When I gave up and ran for the car I realized that in spite of three days of excellent fishing the Suir had had the final say and presented me with a challenge that I had failed to meet successfully.

17
THE TEIGN

FOR MORE THAN a dozen years I have lived in the valley of the upper Teign on the edge of Dartmoor and in that time I have come to know and understand it more than any other stream. Even for an angler who enjoys travelling near and far in search of trout, there is something very special about acquiring an intimate knowledge of a stretch of river in a way that can only be done by living in close proximity to it.

The Teign that I know best is the lengthy stretch from Chagford down to Steps Bridge, much of which is controlled by the Upper Teign Fishing Association, and this is where the best of the trout fishing is to be found. Certainly there are plenty of trout throughout the river, but the lower Teign is primarily a salmon and sea-trout stream and relatively little trout fishing is done.

From time to time, a salmon fisherman will drop his worm into a pocket between the boulders and out will come a brown trout of two, three or even four pounds. The fly fisher, however, should not be fooled by such a happening, as most anglers have never taken a brown trout in excess of a pound from the Teign. The river's great strength is its head of fish from eight to ten inches, with the odd trout up to twelve inches, but beyond that size any trout taken on a fly is either a monster or a sea trout that has been in the river for some time.

The problem is that for every trout over eight inches there is a substantially larger number of fish below that length, and newcomers find it difficult to take the better fish with any consistency. In fact, I hear all too often of anglers who fish for a whole season without catching a decent fish. Yes, the Teign can be a difficult and frustrating river, but one which well repays time spent in getting to know and understand it.

WOODED GORGE

The upper Teign splits neatly into two parts – the water above Castle Drogo and that below. The upper part wanders quietly through the meadows around Chagford, a small stream with plenty of trout, but the smooth surface and clear water can make the fishing very difficult. Below Drogo, the Teign becomes more rocky and quicker as it flows through a deep wooded gorge past Fingle Bridge and Clifford Bridge, all the way down to Steps Bridge. This is one of the great beauty spots of Devon, so that means that you share the river with the many visitors who come to walk the riverside paths.

The early days of the season will see the occasional good hatch of dark olives, but these are very much the exception, and the often considerable numbers of grannom in April are usually ignored by the trout. This means that a well sunk wet fly does best in the early weeks, but by late April or early May the dry fly begins to earn its keep. The combination of wooded banks and fast water creates an ideal habitat for the black gnat and in May and early June these insects swarm over the Teign in huge numbers and produce prolonged rises from the trout. In fact, this is only the start of the terrestrial activity which is so important on this river. Wood ants, beetles and caterpillars provide a constant flow of food from the trees that are virtually unbroken on both banks of the river.

The deep wooded valley below Drogo is also ideal for providing day-long fishing on the brightest day, even in summer, and I have often found the trout less accommodating on a dull day and in the evening. Upstream in the meadows is the best bet for a big evening rise, especially in the season of the consistent blue-winged olive. As a general rule it pays to fish the gorge in the day and the meadows in the evening.

The trees that provide cover and food for the trout make it virtually impossible to fish from the bank on the Teign, except on the big open weir pools which are a virtual waste of time and tempt the beginner into spending countless hours trying to lure trout that are easily seen but almost impossible to catch. If ever there was a river where wading was essential it is the Teign and I use body waders more often than thigh waders on this river, even though its rocky bottom calls for careful wading.

An outing in 1990 on the upper Teign near my home brought together the daytime fishing of late spring and the evening fishing of summer in a single day. It was 7 June, at the beginning of that long, hot summer, and, although we were not to know it at the time, the streams were to shrink to exceptionally low levels and stay that way for the rest of the season.

In early June, however, the Teign was still at an ideal fishing level and the bright if rather cool morning promised every likelihood of good fishing. In the deep, wooded valley around Fingle Bridge the sun is late to penetrate right down to the river, even with the approach of midsummer, so it was ten o'clock before I drove the short distance of less than a mile down to the car-park, just over the bridge.

BLACK GNAT

Over the past four weeks the dominant fly on the water had been the black gnat, so I tied on my usual poly-wing dressing. Having decided to fish upstream, I walked up the riverside footpath past Fingle Weir for nearly half a mile to Black Pool. The lower half of this pool is slow and fairly deep, a spot which often holds salmon, but the top half is quick and shallow, ideal for the dry fly.

It was immediately apparent that the black gnat activity was in decline, with only a fraction of the insects that had been hovering over the stream a week earlier. Nevertheless, several fish were already rising, and as I worked up the pool I managed to pick off three browns of seven to eight inches.

THE GREEN CATERPILLAR

The next pool upstream, however, was devoid of apparent activity and I always like to see the odd rising trout when fishing the black gnat. Several olive uprights lifted from the stream, and a few sedges were fluttering over the river, but the sight that excited my interest was a little green caterpillar descending from a branch on a gossamer thread. On my last visit to the Teign, a few days earlier, I had noticed a small number of these caterpillars, a welcome sight after several years with hardly any to be seen. I remembered well the fabulous fishing of nearly a decade earlier, when the caterpillars reached near-plague proportions for several years and drove the trout to a feeding frenzy. Since then, the population had plummeted.

A careful search in the riverside trees revealed a number of the small bright-green caterpillars, each less than an inch long. So, deciding that it was worth a try, I tied on the simple dressing that had worked so well in the past.

The best water for fishing the caterpillar is the exact opposite of that which suits the dry fly. While the quick, broken, shallower stretches usually work best when fishing dry, it is on the slow, smooth stretches, which can otherwise be all but impossible, that the caterpillar works best. Even the very thin water right at the tail of the pool should be fished, and that was where I made my first cast.

Being slightly heavy, the caterpillar drops with a distinct plop, and this can really excite the trout once they have developed a taste for the creatures. The fish usually respond immediately the fly hits the water, and such was the case on this occasion, with a boil and a pull at the first cast. Three casts later and a fish was well hooked, a trout which proved to be eleven inches long – a good fish for the upper Teign. Having taken two more fish from the pool, I became aware of two club members who had been quietly watching. They asked if I would mind if they watched the caterpillar technique for a while, so we strolled upstream to the next suitable pool.

There is a series of beautiful pools below the granite outline of Sharp Tor, and I slipped into the water just below the tail of the lowest of these. My first cast into a few inches of water produced a huge boil, and in seconds all the spare line was gone from my left hand and the reel was screaming. At that moment I had visions of easily winning the Association's trout trophy, if only

TYING THE GREEN CATERPILLAR

Any caterpillars that fall upon the water are likely to be taken by the trout, but that of the green oak tortrix moth can cause particular excitement when present in large numbers. Tying an effective imitation could hardly be easier, as all you really need is some light-green wool wrapped round the shank of a hook.

HOOK: *10 or 12 standard wet-fly hook, or Partridge longshank Caddis, code K12ST, size 14. The hook sizes in this range are rather odd, and the 14 looks about the same as a size 10*
BODY: *Light-green wool or dubbed fur, started well into the bend*
RIB: *Fine copper wire. Virtually any ribbing will do, as its main purpose is to prolong the life of the fly*

Although this pattern can be extremely effective when the natural is present, it is likely to be ignored by trout at other times and I have even seen trout become very agitated at its presence.

this fish would stay hooked. I gained a little line and then the fish was off again, but the next time I gained line I saw a silvery flash in the clear water and knew that this was no resident brown. Shortly after, I slipped the net under a sixteen-inch sea trout, removed the barbless hook and slid him back into the stream. My audience was suitably impressed by my stroke of good luck.

I fished on upstream for a further half-mile, and every pool produced a fish or two. By early afternoon, the fish were still rushing at the caterpillar, but more and more were failing actually to take it. When I decided to call a halt soon after two o'clock, a dozen trout over eight inches and numerous smaller fish had been caught and released, the best brown being the eleven-incher.

EVENING RETURN

After an afternoon in the garden, I decided to return to the river in the evening, to take advantage of the blue-winged olives, which had started

BELOW Teign brown: caterpillar green.

hatching early in the 1990 season. This time I drove the two miles to Mill End Bridge and walked downstream for about three-quarters of a mile. I find that distance just about right to fish back to the car in a couple of hours. The fact that the Teign runs out of the west at this point can be a distinct advantage when you want to fish late. The setting sun can be a problem at first, but casting into the dying light after sunset can extend the fishing by half an hour, and there is something very special about casting to rises in the reflected light of the afterglow, when all else is almost dark.

By half past seven I was ready to fish and, although the real rise had yet to start, a few small trout were jumping at the odd sedge fluttering near the surface. In the pre-rise period, a sedge cast into the quick broken water will often move a few trout, so I tied on the simple no-hackle hairwing sedge that had lured many trout for me in such conditions. In the next three-quarters of an hour plenty of trout came splashing at the sedge. Most were small, but three in the eight-to-nine-inch class were netted and released.

SHERRY SPINNERS

Then, around a quarter-past eight, the sherry spinners began to gather over the river, and the first began to drift down on the surface after laying their eggs. Few types of insect activity are more likely to spur a rise than a fall of sherry spinners, and this occasion was no exception. Soon the smoother pools were alive with dimpling fish, steadily feeding on the dead and dying insects.

This may be one of the great fishing opportunities, but all too often it can prove a disappointment. Those spinners are lying flat on the surface, and that is where your imitation has to be if you want to get full value from the rise – yet few anglers on rain-fed rivers carry spinner imitations. The poly-wing spinner I use is easy to tie, floats flat on the surface and is a great fish catcher.

Even if you have the right dressing, careful presentation can be the key to success, as a drag-free drift is essential – dead insects do not move, other than with the current. Your other problem is that the light is dying and time is fast running out, so it is all too easy to become hasty and start casting raggedly, get a tangle, and the rot sets in.

On that June evening I kept fishing into the dying light until half past ten, and took fifteen more trout between eight and eleven inches, as well as the inevitable tiddlers that you are bound to catch on a natural fishery. Although the blue-winged olive duns hatched late in the evening, I stuck with the spinner and had no cause to regret the decision.

It had been a good day, but by no means the best that early June can provide. The great charm of this period is the variety of insects that hatch, and the need to change your techniques as the day progresses.

18
THE DART

THE SUN HAD dropped behind the high moors and soon it would be sea-trout time, but for the time being it was still the brown trout that were occupying my attention. It was a warm August evening on the West Dart above Hexworthy and the fall of sherry spinners in the past hour had produced plenty of wild moorland trout, though nothing over twelve inches. Then, in the thin water at the head of the pool, the water bulged as a good fish rose and then rose again. I dropped the size 14 Pheasant Tail two feet above the rising fish, waited the agonizing couple of seconds as it drifted back to the fish, struck as the fly was sucked under and suddenly I was playing something much bigger than I had anticipated. Good fortune was on my side and eventually I slipped the net under a twenty-inch brown trout that just failed by an ounce to make three pounds. That experience was back in 1975 and really brought home to me just how big the trout can be on the moorland reaches of the Dart.

The Dart was the first river that I fished after arriving in Devon twenty years ago and I have fished it countless times since – and all on one fishery. To be confined to one fishery may sound like an imposition but in this case the water in question is the extensive fishery of the Duchy of Cornwall, which covers most of the Dart system above Dartmeet, where the East and West Dart join. Not only does the fishery include the East and West Dart but also the main tributaries – Swincombe Brook, Cherry Brook, Walla Brook, Black Brook and Cowsic Brook. This really is the place for the angler who likes to explore mile after mile of river and who enjoys the challenge of variety.

THE DUCHY FISHERY

The largest river of the Duchy fishery is the West Dart and the cream of the fishing on this big stream is probably from Huccaby Bridge up to Prince Hall. This stretch has some impressive pools which are much favoured by salmon and sea-trout anglers but, although they hold some big trout, they can easily lead the trout fisher into wasting much time for meagre results. The smooth, deep water offers little to the fly fisher seeking trout, except perhaps in the

ABOVE High up the West Dart at Prince Hall.
OPPOSITE Cherry Brook: a tributary of the West Dart.

late evening, and it is best to confine yourself to a few casts in the broken water at the head of each pool.

Far more promising are the other two types of water which are readily available on the West Dart. First there is the steady run of broken water, perhaps two to three feet deep, ideal for both wet and dry fly. One such run just above the mouth of Swincombe Brook has rarely failed to produce a trout or two and on one sparkling spring day my dry Dark Olive was taken by a fish of nearly two pounds at the head of the run.

The West Dart also has several stretches which are broken up by numerous large boulders, and these provide cover for a large population of trout. On such a stretch, it is possible to get close to each pocket among the boulders without frightening the trout. The boulders that provide cover for the trout also hide the approach of the angler from downstream, and when a dry fly is dropped onto the pocket there is always a good chance that a trout will appear and grab it.

T H E   E A S T   D A R T

The East Dart is a much smaller stream but also holds plenty of trout. Indeed, it was on the tiny headwaters way above Postbridge that I took my best East Dart trout on a bright, cold Easter Day. I walked about a mile upstream from Postbridge and tackled up with a couple of wet flies – a Greenwell on the point and a Grizzle Palmer on the dropper. There was nothing hatching and a dry fly would probably have been whisked away from the surface in the gusting wind. For the first mile upstream the trout came steadily to the fly, but most were small, with only one fish about nine inches. Then as I cast over a strand of barbed wire that crossed the stream, into a shallow pool, the water bulged as a big fish swung round and followed my dropper fly downstream, plucked at it tantalizingly and was gone.

The brief glimpse that I had was enough to mark that fish for future attention, so I skirted the pool and fished on upstream for another hour. Then I moved back to renew my encounter with the big fish, and again cast over the barbed wire into the pool. Three casts with the wet flies produced no response, so I changed to a single dry Dark Olive, size 16, and cast it hopefully onto the pool. This time the response was immediate as the fly disappeared to a lunging rise and in seconds the fish had rushed downstream, I had passed the rod under the barbed wire, and the action had moved to the pool below. With more space to play with it was only a matter of time before the well hooked fish was drawn onto the gravel and I was admiring a heavily-spotted seventeen-inch brown before slipping it back into the stream.

T I N Y   T R I B U T A R I E S

Some of the most fascinating fishing on Dartmoor is on the tiny tributaries, all of which have given me splendid fishing in their different ways. On the Swincombe, many years ago, I recall guiding Sid Neff and putting him in touch with a sixteen-inch trout that took his dry fly in a pocket only a yard across. The Cherry Brook, especially on the stretch between the two roads that cross it, is ideal dry-fly water, but it was on Black Brook that I enjoyed my best ever dry-fly fishing on the moor. It was a dull, still July afternoon and I had fished up the West Dart from Prince Hall, a stretch that is normally productive but on this occasion produced only two small trout for my efforts. By the time I reached the mouth of Black Brook my enthusiasm was definitely waning and I decided to fish up the tributary for half an hour before giving up. Even as I moved into Black Brook a couple of blue-winged olives drifted by and within minutes the trickle had turned into a flood of duns coming down the stream.

Suddenly the stream was transformed, with trout rising eagerly where minutes before the surface had been unbroken. The lower Black Brook is a smooth stream with little broken water, with the shallower water carrying much more weed than is normal on the moor, and it was in the runs and pockets between the weeds that the trout had settled down to feeding steadily on the blue-winged olives. Indeed, but for the moorland surroundings, the scene could easily have been on a chalk stream. As usual in a daytime hatch of blue-winged olives, it was the fly with the yellowish-olive body that worked well and in less than two hours eighteen trout from eight to fourteen inches had transformed that dull July afternoon into a treasured memory.

A superb series of pools on the West Dart.

19
THE OTTER AND THE CULM

LONG BEFORE MOVING to Devon in 1970 I had read much about perhaps its most famous trout stream, the Otter. Stories of dry-fly fishing in the chalkstream style had excited my imagination so, by the time I found myself within easy reach of this lovely river, it was a great disappointment to find that it had slipped from its former glory. Certainly, it still held plenty of trout, but not in the quality or numbers of its great days, and much of the available fishing was maintained only by stocking with fish of keepable size.

So for nearly twenty years my introduction to the Otter was delayed, perhaps above all because of a lesser-known stream which runs a parallel course through the same lowland farm country of east Devon – the Culm. Like the Otter, the Culm rises in the Blackdown Hills, but quickly drops into its broad valley and runs most of its course through level meadows and looks exactly what it is – a classic little trout stream.

For half a dozen years I lived in the valley of the lower Culm and there the river is primarily a coarse fishery, but it was necessary to drive only a few miles upstream to find excellent dry-fly fishing for trout of good average size. The best of this fishing was from Hemyock down to Uffculme and fortunately there were two stretches that could be fished simply by the purchase of a day permit. The stretch that I plumped for was that at Uffculme – a fortunate choice which produced some wonderful trout fishing during my time in the Culm valley, and which still draws me back for the odd day each season.

Of all the Devon streams that I fish it is on the Culm that I have probably enjoyed the most varied and prolific insect hatches, from April days with brief hatches of dark olives, through the peak hatches in May culminating in the mayfly itself, to the prolonged activity during the summer evening hatches of blue-winged olives. Yet the Culm is a coloured, almost muddy stream, with never the clarity of the chalk streams to the east or the moorland rivers to the west. Undoubtedly it suffers from the pollution that is virtually inevitable on any stream that runs through intensively farmed country, and most stretches have little weed, yet somehow the Culm provides a habitat for large numbers of trout and the insects that bring them to the surface.

The stretch above Uffculme that I came to know so well had just about

Deer Park Hotel water on the Otter near Honiton, Devon.

every type of water that makes fly fishing so fascinating – small boulder weirs, gravel runs, deep undercut banks, the odd deep pool, and even a stretch where it splits into two little streams for nearly half a mile. It was particularly in the long days of late spring and early summer, when there always seems to be something happening on the stream, that I gained an intimate knowledge of the Culm and enjoyed countless hours of enjoyment. One day towards the end of spring showed the Culm at its very best.

A DAY IN MAY

It was, in fact, the twenty-fourth day of May and when I parked my car by the river at Uffculme the mid-morning sun was already promising a warm day. For the first few hundred yards of my walk upstream there was no sign of hatching fly or rising fish and then, in the smooth run above a small weir, I saw the first movement. Shortly the trout rose again, and then again, and I became aware of the first hatching pale wateries leaving the water and rising in the still air. Those first few duns soon became a hatch of considerable proportions and that first rising trout was quickly joined by three more fish over a stretch of no more than six yards.

My first cast with a size 18 Pale Watery Dun was ignored, as were the next twenty casts, even though the trout continued to rise steadily. I could only assume that these fish were taking the emerging insects, so I quickly changed to a size 18 emerger, with a tan body and vestigial wings of pale blue dun hackle tips little more than an eighth of an inch long. Instead of being cocked up on its hackles, the emerger drifted down right in the surface film and that was exactly what those trout wanted. The first fish of eleven inches was followed by a dozen more between eight and twelve inches during the hour-long duration of the hatch. All took the emerger solidly, with not a fish coming adrift.

Soon after noon, the hatch of pale wateries had petered out, and, although the odd olive upright was hatching, it was the black gnat that had become dominant, with swarms over all the more broken water. Now it was the turn of a size 18 Black Gnat to deliver the goods, as it did superbly for the next couple of hours. By then I had reached the junction at the bottom of the stretch where the river splits into two branches and, as I moved into the right branch, I became aware that here black gnats were virtually absent. But on that wonderful day my luck was in and soon the first few mayflies came drifting down the narrow sidestream, so on went a simple hackle pattern.

The very first cast to a rise under an overhanging bush attracted a good fish and, although it tried hard to get among the trailing brambles, eventually a trout of well over a pound was netted and released. That was a foretaste to two more hours of hectic sport until just after four o'clock. Although all of the day's catch had been returned, I had been keeping a careful check of any fish over eight inches and with the total at forty-two it seemed appropriate to bring the proceedings to a close. It was my forty-second birthday.

MAYFLY HATCH

A week later I returned at the height of the mayfly hatch and this time I had no reason to use any other fly – first the dun and then, towards evening, the spinner. The thing that made that day stand out was an excursion up the Culm's tributary, the Craddock Brook. Normally, I never fished the brook but at mayfly time it often enjoyed the most prolific hatches, for its muddy bed provided ideal habitat for the mayfly larvae. When I reached the mouth of the brook I was immediately aware of a stream of mayflies flowing out into the main river and every tiny pool in the bottom half-mile of the brook revealed rising trout just waiting for a mayfly to be cast to them.

My most recent visit to the Culm was on 29 May 1990, when I made a start a mile above Uffculme on a straight stretch of a hundred yards where one bank is protected from erosion by neat stonework constructed many years ago. The deeper water is tight against the stonework and it is there that the current brings the flies down to the waiting trout. It was an unsettled day, with light rain first, then a dry spell, and then heavy rain, but a few mayflies were hatching so I tied on a hackle pattern with a pink body. It seemed to be what they wanted and the first cast produced a ten-incher, followed by two more to thirteen inches. A short excursion up the Craddock Brook added two more brownies to the bag and then, as I fished the pool in the main river at the mouth of the brook, I was suddenly into a bright silver fish that clattered all around the pool until it was netted. To my surprise, it proved to be a nine-inch rainbow, my first ever from the Culm, and it was soon followed by two more of thirteen and fourteen inches. All were in excellent condition with unblemished tails that suggested they had been in the stream for a considerable time, taking on the appearance and characteristics of wild fish. It has become almost a reflex action to condemn the presence of rainbow trout in streams, whether the result of stocking or escapes from hatcheries, but these were fish that I would have been happy to catch at any time in any place.

By early afternoon a hatch of blue-winged olives had started – a hatch which developed through the afternoon into the biggest emergence of the fly that I have ever seen that early in the season. It was the mayfly, however, that brought the trout most readily to my fly and when heavy rain in the late afternoon drove me from the river the catch had reached ten browns and eight rainbows, topped by a fourteen-incher of each species.

FIRST VISIT

It was inevitable that eventually I would get around to the Otter and my first real experience of the river was on the last day of May in 1990, when I accepted Steve Noar's invitation to try out the fishing at the Deer Park Hotel near Honiton. A couple of years before I had seen the stream improvement carried out by Steve and Gilbert Barratt, with the creation and restoration of weirs to provide more holding water and the strengthening of banks against erosion. Unfortunately, the thing they had not been able to control was the water quality, and reports indicated that stream-bred trout were in short supply throughout the Otter. I knew that the Deer Park fishery was well stocked with hatchery fish, but I was hoping that I might still be able to find a wild trout or two.

After a mid-morning briefing from Gilbert over coffee in the hotel lounge, we went down to the river, where I saw plenty of evidence of further improvements since my previous visit. Perhaps the most encouraging sign was the abundance of nymphs under the fly boards that were moored to one

The Culm: prolific insect hatches, yet a coloured almost muddy stream.

of the small weirs – far, far more than under the stones on the stream bed.

Time passed quickly and it was well past noon before I made the first cast of the day. A walk along the river had revealed very little fly and only the occasional rise, but when a fish rose three times just off some bankside reeds I decided that it was worth a try. As there was no hatch of fly, I tied on one of my favourites in such conditions, a hackle Adams. The fish was lying just upstream of quickening water at the tail of the pool, so a long cast would clearly leave the bulk of the line lying on water faster than that where the fly would alight, resulting in instant drag. The only answer was to take the fish from close quarters so I slipped into the stream and waded slowly and carefully to within five yards of the rising trout. By holding the rod high, I could now easily drift the fly over the fish without drag and a fourteen-inch stocked brown came at the first cast.

The next fish was rising in boiling and twisting water created by boulders that had been set in place for bank protection, so once again a close approach was necessary to ensure that the minimum length of fly line was on the water. The tactic paid off again with another fourteen-inch fish. Before a break for lunch, two more rising trout were spotted and both came to the Adams, but contact with both fish was brief.

After a break I was back on the water by three o'clock, still looking for my first wild fish. Two more stocked browns came quickly, one of them off the same bankside boulders where I had caught a fish earlier. One particularly good fish was rising tight against the bank just above the spot where a small bush pushed the current out towards the middle of the stream. The bush made it impossible to cast from downstream so I tried to drift the fly down from above, but it always skated just before reaching the fish and put it down. Three times I returned after an interval and found that trout rising again, and three more times I put it down.

Then, just when I was thinking of packing up, I found two fish rising in the smooth water just above a little weir and both took the Adams first time. Although of modest size, both fought savagely, so it was no surprise when they proved to be bright wild fish of ten and eleven inches, a high note on which to end the day.

There is no doubt that the Otter has a long way to go, but this lovely little river deserves any effort to restore it to its former position as a trout stream. I certainly look forward to fishing it again and then I hope to see an increase in the number of wild trout in the catch.

20

THE EXE
AND ITS TRIBUTARIES

MY FIRST ENCOUNTER with the Exe was in the heart of Exmoor, where the infant stream tumbles down from the moor through a series of tiny pools. At first glance, it appeared too small to hold anything worth catching, but those pools were often deeper than they looked and there were plenty of boulders and rocky overhangs to provide cover. It was May, with the newly born lambs in the streamside meadows and the new leaves on the trees giving a wonderful sense of freshness in that lovely Exmoor valley.

I was staying at Westermill Farm, which owns a lengthy stretch of the Exe. Around the farm, the stream runs through small meadows with plenty of bankside cover but a mile or so upstream it breaks out onto the moor and becomes increasingly open. This is ideal-looking water for working up the stream with a small buoyant dry fly, a promise that was fulfilled on that visit of long ago, with eager moorland trout appearing from nowhere to take my offering. Most were between six and eight inches, but the deeper pools produced several colourful brownies up to nine inches and one only just fell short of being a monster of ten inches.

From those tiny upland reaches, the Exe grows slowly as it flows its wooded course down past the village of Winsford, takes in the Haddeo and then its major tributary, the Barle, near Dulverton. Above the mouth of the Barle it is often called the Little Exe, but once the extra water comes in from the Barle the Exe becomes a major stream and flows through a broad and impressive valley past Tiverton to Exeter and the sea.

MEMORABLE CATCHES

It was around Tiverton that I enjoyed my next experience of the Exe. For several years I lived close enough to be a member of the Tiverton Fly Fishing Club, which has water above and below the town. I fished both stretches, but it was the water downstream towards Bickleigh that I came to know best and which produced some memorable catches.

Although it produced fish for me at a variety of times, it is for the evening fishing that I remember this fishery best. The short walk from the car-park gave access to the bottom of the water, where it ran wide and shallow, but only a couple of hundred yards upstream it deepened and became a long, slow tree-lined pool of more than a quarter of a mile. Normally this pool was quite dead, without a sign of a rising trout, but whenever there was a hatch its huge head of fish was revealed, with countless rises breaking the calm surface.

The insects which brought about these rises, at least in my experience, were sedges and blue-winged olives. The best of the sedge hatch was surprisingly early in the season, in late May, when at dusk the big fluttering flies skated across the surface and the trout rushed at them with those explosive rises that are so exciting. In the dying light, a hairwing sedge dragged across the surface could hardly fail and most evenings saw the catch topped by trout of a pound or better.

The problem with sedge fishing, however, is that it all happens so quickly with little time to savour the normal delights of dry-fly fishing. Very exciting, but all a bit frantic for my taste. The long summer evenings of June and July were altogether another matter, with the prolonged activity of the fall of sherry spinner and the hatch of blue-winged olive providing two hours or more of intensely enjoyable fishing. On the best evenings, the rises in that long pool would often be so numerous that they almost looked like rain and the trout would come eagerly to a well presented Sherry Spinner. Both banks of the pool had an impenetrable line of trees which put bank fishing quite out of the question, but with my body waders it was possible to wade carefully up the middle of the stream, putting every rising trout within reach. As none of the other members appeared to have body waders, I never had to share that pool with another angler, and it was quite normal to catch and release twenty or more fish during an evening.

THE BARLE

Unfortunately, opportunities to fish the middle Exe are very limited, most of the water being preserved for salmon fishing, but for the visitor the position is much brighter on the Barle where three hotel fisheries offer many miles of good trout fishing. Possibly the best known is the Carnarvon Arms, which controls several miles of water on both the Exe and the Barle, and it was there that I fished the Barle for the first time.

It was the first day of May and I had driven up to Wimbleball Reservoir for the opening of the season. Normally I really enjoy my visits to Wimbleball but this time there was a howling cold wind, and after a couple of hours I decided that I would rather be somewhere more comfortable.

I drove to the Carnarvon Arms near Dulverton and luckily the bottom beat on the Barle was free. It was like entering another world, with only a gentle breeze penetrating the valley, and for the first time that day I felt the warmth of the sun. So, too, did the river, as a trickle of olives was drifting downstream and the odd fish was breaking surface.

My enthusiasm was instantly rekindled and, after wading carefully into position, I dropped a size 16 imitation of a dark olive over the nearest fish. It responded immediately and proved to be a trout of ten inches. As I slipped it back into the river, I was aware of another rise about six yards upstream and again the fish took first cast. This time the line hissed through the water as the fish rushed downstream past me and it took some time to work it back up to the net. This was a lovely brown trout of about a pound – probably a stocked fish, but I was in the mood to be happy with anything that came my way.

LEFT "Then at the fourth attempt there was a gentle sip and at once I saw the cause of this unusual behaviour - a grayling."

BELOW Wading a wooded stretch of the Barle above Tarr Steps.

A S U R P R I S E G R A Y L I N G

Despite my catching two decent fish, the odd rise was still to be seen, one of them barely a couple of yards across the stream. So close, indeed, that it was a case of dropping the fly over it rather than casting to it. I was immediately aware of a vertical shadow drifting downstream below the fly, but no take was forthcoming. The same thing happened with the next two casts and then at the fourth attempt there was a gentle sip and at once I saw the cause of this unusual behaviour – a grayling. I had forgotten that the Exe system holds a fair number of grayling, but was delighted to renew my acquaintance with a species which I have enjoyed so much in the past, but fished for only infrequently since I went to live in the south-west.

It was a good fish, too, all of a pound, and that same pool produced one more of similar size before both trout and grayling decided that things had gone a bit too far and stopped rising.

Although that first pool provided the best of the fishing, there were always fish to be caught that afternoon and a very pleasant two hours produced four good grayling and seven trout.

My next visit to the Barle was a month later in very different conditions and on a very different stretch. It was early June and warmer weather had arrived. I was fishing at Tarr Steps, where the Tarr Steps Hotel controls some four miles of boulder-strewn river running through a deep wooded valley. The sun was out, the black gnats were swarming in countless numbers over the fast stretches, and conditions were ideal for exploring with a light rod and a small fly. I was using my normal Black Gnat pattern comprising a black fur body, white poly wing and black hackle, size 18.

Not surprisingly on such a fine day, the meadow at Tarr Steps, a famous Exmoor beauty spot, was rather busy but a short walk upstream left the trippers behind. Over the next three hours I worked gradually upstream, fishing all the likely spots for well over a mile. There are few certainties in fishing but one of the things that you can bank on is that a fine day in the black gnat season will nearly always produce good fishing on the moorland rivers of the south-west, especially on the fast-flowing wooded reaches.

That day was no exception and trout after trout came to the fly. In the fast water many were missed and many others threw the hook, but over thirty fish up to twelve inches were caught and released. Although the first sedges of summer were on the water and a few upwinged flies were hatching, insect activity was dominated by the millions of black gnats and I needed to change the fly only when it became sodden or bedraggled.

T H E H A D D E O

The Haddeo is a delightful little tributary that meanders through a wooded valley for the few miles from the dam at Wimbleball down to its confluence with the Exe. Drive a couple of miles up the valley, away from the main road in the Exe valley, and the sense of remoteness is complete. I had fished the bottom half-mile of the Haddeo a couple of times when fishing the Little Exe at Pixton, but it was not until May 1990 that I explored the remote upper valley and then I enjoyed a remarkable session in unusual conditions.

By late May, the 1990 drought was well established and most rivers in the south-west were reduced to a trickle, with fishing becoming increasingly difficult. A report from the National Rivers Authority had revealed that the Torridge was running at only 13 per cent of normal and few rivers were faring much better. Then I recalled that the Haddeo was used as a conduit for the water being fed from Wimbleball Reservoir into the Exe to provide water for extraction downstream, so perhaps there I would find more promising conditions. A quick call to John Sharpe, who managed the Haddeo, revealed that it was free, so on a hot sunny afternoon I drove up the lonely valley and parked by the stream.

The first glance at the river revealed that it was running full, clear and cold, a revelation compared with the other rivers in the area. Indeed, when I waded into the stream I was amazed by the force of the current and the coldness coming through my waders. The stretch that I had chosen meanders through small meadows, with the steep wooded slopes of the valley never more than a hundred yards away, and even as I started I saw the welcome sight of a few mayfly fluttering across the meadows. As nothing else was hatching, I tied on my usual hackle pattern and, although there was no sign of rising fish, the trout were clearly waiting for food as the first cast produced a splashing rise. As the afternoon progressed the hatch of mayfly increased, and soon trout were rising in all the larger pools, and I enjoyed two hours of easy and productive fishing with thirteen browns to eleven inches.

Dams may have a lot to answer for, with the drowning of valleys and the destruction of runs of migratory fish, but on that May afternoon I had been able to enjoy one beneficial result of the need to build reservoirs.

21
THE LYN

As I slipped into the water at the tail of Meadow Pool, I could hardly believe the sight before me. This pool always held a large head of fish, but usually the smooth surface and crystal-clear water made it difficult to take more than a fish or two before the rest became unsettled and started milling around in the way that tells you that further fishing is pointless.

On this occasion, however, everything was very different. Every fish in the pool appeared to be just below the surface, constantly sipping in the flies that formed a virtual haze over the water.

At the first cast with the tiny dry fly, a nine-inch fish took without hesitation and, when I left the pool some twenty minutes later, a dozen wild brown trout to eleven inches had been caught and released. That was the start of a wonderful day's fishing, and on virtually every pool and pocket it was possible to take several trout before the disturbance eventually made it necessary to move on.

The river where this took place was the East Lyn, the short Devon river that brings together several tiny Exmoor streams – Chalk Water, Weir Water, Badgeworthy Water, Oare Water – and then rushes down to the sea at Lynmouth. The place was Rockford, the fly on the water was the black gnat, and the time was early June. On this particular occasion the trout kept feeding throughout the day, first on black gnat and later on sedge, until from sheer tiredness I called it a day. By then the day's catch had topped eighty, with the best fish close to twelve inches.

SUNSHINE WATER

That may have been an outstanding day, but good days on the Lyn are the rule rather than the exception – especially when the sun shines. Yes, the Lyn really is a sunshine water, where the brighter the day the better the rise. Indeed, I know of no river in Devon where the trout rise more freely than on the East Lyn. Pick a sunny day, in May or June especially, and you can expect to enjoy some of the best dry-fly fishing for wild brown trout in the south-west.

RIGHT Among the boulders: dappled light on the East Lyn.

Fortunately, this fishing is available for all to enjoy, as the Glenthorne and Watersmeet fisheries, which run from Brendon down to the sea at Lynmouth, are controlled by the National Rivers Authority, who issue unlimited permits at a very reasonable cost.

Even as you arrive at the river, the trout are usually advertising their presence. If you park your car at Rockford, a tiny North Devon village, and cross the footbridge, the fish are lined up below taking any insects that come their way. I can never resist dangling a fly over them to see how they react, and most other anglers succumb to this temptation. Indeed, this often accounts for the first fish or two of the day.

Above Rockford: dry fly on the Lyn.

CASCADES AND POOLS

Below Rockford, the Lyn plunges into its dramatic wooded gorge with a series of cascades and pools all the way to Lynmouth. The big pools are all full of fish but it is best not to spend too much time over the trout which are easily seen cruising in the slow deep water. You can see them but they can also see you and, although they will move away only if you become too intrusive, they are sufficiently on their guard to be virtually uncatchable. Stick to the quicker broken water near the head of the pool where you can approach the trout more easily without being seen; they are also usually bigger and easier to catch.

Above Rockford, the valley broadens slightly, with little riverside meadows, and here you will find some of the very best dry-fly fishing, along a series of narrow runs and small pools. In many places, the main current runs tight along the steep rocky bank and here the fish line up waiting for the insects that come down on the current.

Perhaps the most productive fishing of all is in the small pockets along the boulder-strewn stretch of river immediately above and below Rockford. Most of these pockets are full of trout and even a pocket only a yard or two square will produce a couple of good fish.

The technique on this fishery is to work upstream with a dry fly, getting in close to the fish. Although this can sometimes be achieved from the bank, there will be many more occasions when wading is essential. With a careful approach, it will rarely be necessary to cast more than six yards, except on a few of the larger pools. With such a rocky bottom, the wading can be tricky, so a wading staff not only cuts out the risk of a ducking but also avoids noisy stumbling which would scare the fish.

Except when a single fly such as the black gnat predominates, which is rare on the Lyn, virtually any dry fly that shows up well works well, but my own preference would be for a Hairwing Sedge, Grey Duster or an Adams, with 16 the normal size.

Dry fly is likely to do best on nine days out of ten, but I remember one summer day when the wet fly came into its own. Heavy rain and reports of a run of salmon had encouraged me to drive up to the Lyn but, by the time I arrived, the river had dropped and cleared, and a couple of hours with the salmon outfit produced nothing. The river was still a bit above normal, running fast with a tinge of colour, so I returned to the car, assembled the trout outfit and tied on a couple of size 14 wet flies – a Silver March Brown on the point and a Soldier Palmer on the dropper.

From the first cast it was clear that the falling river had induced a suicidal mood in the trout. As I fished a short line across and downstream through the pools around Rockford, fish came rushing at the flies with complete abandon, and on several occasions two trout were taken at a time. The best taking time as a moorland stream drops after a flood may be short-lived, but if you can be on the river when it happens you are never likely to enjoy easier fishing.

'I walked downstream, deep into Monsal Dale'.

22
THE DERBYSHIRE WYE

UNTIL ABOUT A hundred years ago the rainbow trout was still restricted to its natural home in the Pacific coast streams of North America and then, in a few short decades, its range expanded dramatically, with the help of man, first to other parts of North America, then to South America, Europe, New Zealand and Australia and eventually to the high country of northern India and Africa. Part of this great artificial migration was to Britain. Yet, after nearly a century of widespread stocking on many rivers and lakes, it has surprisingly failed to become a successful self-sustaining species as it has in so many other parts of the world.

Over the years, the rainbow has certainly had its opportunities to become established in Britain. No species of trout is easier to rear to catchable size in a fish farm, or cheaper to produce, so artificial stocking of rainbows has been carried out on a large scale, especially as a result of the dramatic growth of small stocked trout ponds in recent years. Indeed, the rainbow forms the basis of stocking on artificial reservoirs and ponds in Britain and the result has been some spectacular fishing for big rainbows. Rivers too have received many plantings of rainbows.

In the early 1970s Dr Winifred Frost, in her paper *A Survey of the Rainbow Trout in Britain and Ireland*, estimated that rainbows were present in more than five hundred waters, and the dramatic growth of small put-and-take trout pools since then has probably taken the figure to well over a thousand. However, if the facts behind that figure are closely examined, they reveal that it is almost impossible to deliberately catch a wild stream-bred rainbow anywhere in Britain. Inevitably, a few stocked rainbows breed naturally from time to time and most experienced anglers will have caught the occasional result of such reproduction. For example, several small chalk streams on the northern edge of London developed localized self-sustaining stocks, but these streams have been virtually engulfed by the suburban growth of the capital.

There is, fortunately, one wonderful exception to this story of failure to reproduce naturally. Right in the heart of England, surrounded by some of our largest industrial cities, there is an oasis of great natural beauty and rural peace, the Peak National Park in Derbyshire.

A CLASSIC LIMESTONE STREAM

Significantly, for the flyfisher, most of this area lies on a bedrock of limestone, and that means trout streams. One of these is the Wye, a classic limestone stream with smooth surface, clear water, weeds waving in the current – and fish. Originally those fish were brown trout and grayling, but then, in 1910, rainbows newly arrived from across the Atlantic were introduced and immediately found the river to their liking. Instead of quickly vanishing as they did on so many English streams, they soon settled in, reproduced successfully and gave us the unique fishing that we enjoy today.

Since their introduction to the Wye, rainbows have colonized some twelve miles of the river from Cressbrook down to the mouth at Rowsley, and most of this water can be fished by the visiting angler. The bottom seven miles, from Rowsley up to Bakewell, is part of the Haddon Hall estate, and tickets are available from the Peacock Hotel. The Chatsworth estate has the four and a half miles from Ashford-in-the-Water up to Cressbrook, and all of this can be fished on season tickets direct from the estate or on day tickets which are available to guests at the Cavendish Hotel, Baslow.

My enthusiasm for catching stream-bred rainbows had been kindled by my first fishing trip to the United States in the late 1970s, and since then the Derbyshire Wye had been on my list of rivers to fish at the first opportunity. However, it was not until the late spring of 1986 that I was able to turn that resolution into practice, and it was with a keen sense of anticipation that I drove north from my Devon home. Although my trip was at the end of May, still more than a touch of winter was hanging about, with a cold wind, heavy rain and the cloud level hardly above the tops of the pylons along the M5 and M6. Indeed, I began to fear that the river might be in full flood, but the Derbyshire limestone had absorbed most of the downpour and the Wye, although high, was still fishable.

MAYFLY NYMPHS

My destination was the Chatsworth estate's Monsal Dale fishery, and my visit has been timed to coincide with the hatch of mayfly. But, as bailiff Tom Richardson told me on arrival, that dreadful cold spring had delayed all life in the river, and hardly a mayfly had hatched at that time. However, he reported that the mayfly nymphs had become active and that the trout, both rainbows and browns, were willing to take a well sunk imitation. I decided to tackle up with a simplified version of the Richard Walker Mayfly Nymph.

As I walked down the riverbank below Upperdale Bridge on that first morning, I realized that it was just as well that I would be using the nymph, as there would have been little chance of casting a big dry mayfly in that fierce downstream gale. But, in spite of the unpromising conditions, those wild rainbows were in a taking mood, and as the nymph drifted a couple of feet down through the first pool there was a steady pull and suddenly I was playing my first wild Wye rainbow. It was not a big fish, perhaps twelve inches, but it fought with surprising power, constantly thumping the rod in a way that left no scope for careless handling, before being netted and released.

The river stayed high for the two days of that visit so I had to stick with the deeply fished nymph, except for a brief period on the second afternoon when the wind dropped, the sun almost broke through the clouds, flies started hatching and a few trout broke the surface. The flies were not mayflies but tiny midges, so I turned to a size 20 Black Midge and took six trout, all rainbows, in that brief half-hour interlude.

In those two days I caught and released thirty-eight trout, of which twenty-two were rainbows, demonstrating the way they coexist with browns on the Wye. Most of the fish were between nine and fourteen inches, but two of the rainbows were taped at seventeen inches, probably nudging two pounds each.

'In a deep, slow pool beneath the viaduct...'

A R E T U R N V I S I T

After that brief interlude with the dry fly, I knew I had to get back to the Wye in more benign conditions. The chance came in July 1988, when I enjoyed three days of great dry-fly fishing there. This time the river was running low and clear, and when I checked in with Tom Richardson at his limestone cottage in Monsal Dale he warned me that the trout fishing had been difficult in the last few days. As I walked downstream in the middle of the morning, I could see why, as few insects were hatching and a walk of half a mile did not

RIGHT A wild Wye rainbow comes to the author's net. The weedbeds are luxuriant on this stretch above Ashford-in-the-Water.

BELOW The pale wateries emerged for two hours as I fished below the crags of Monsal Dale.

reveal a single rising trout. Then, in a deep, slow pool beneath the nineteenth-century railway viaduct that now carries the Monsal Trail footpath, I spotted several rising fish. In the slow pool these fish were cruising in all directions, so the problem was anticipating where to drop the fly. Only a few midges were on the water, so I tied on a size 20 Black Midge and, with the aid of polaroids, did my best to place it in the path of one of the cruising trout. Several times fish frustratingly changed direction just before reaching the midge, but once a trout saw the fly it would sip it in without hesitation. The result of perseverance was two rainbows and a brown from the pool.

Throughout the middle of that day, only perhaps one pool in five had rising fish, but once I found them those trout were very willing to take the little midge. This was a day when exploring a lengthy stretch of river really paid off, underlining the fact that it so often pays to go walkabout when trout fishing.

After resting in the afternoon, I returned to the river above the village of Ashford-in-the-Water at seven o'clock full of anticipation – my expectations fired by what I had seen the previous evening when I arrived in Derbyshire. That arrival had been too late for any fishing, but I had stopped by the bridge at Bakewell, where the river was covered with the rises of browns and rainbows taking the hatching blue-winged olives.

S E D G E S   S W A R M I N G

My anticipation was not to be disappointed. Already sedges were swarming over the water and the first few blue-winged olive duns were emerging. The slashing rises of the trout indicated that they were taking sedge and a size 16 hairwing imitation quickly took three trout to fourteen inches. Then the blue-winged olive emergence really took over and the trout settled to sipping in the countless duns drifting down on the current, so I snipped off the sedge and tied on a blue-winged olive imitation. The next hour was terrific and, though a steady drizzle quickly turned to heavy rain, the trout continued to rise even when the surface was whipped up by the torrent. When I ran for the car with the water dripping down my neck, I had caught and released nine rainbows and six browns between ten and fifteen inches.

The second day on the Wye started wet and stayed that way, but I had driven north to fish so I tackled up at 11 a.m. and walked downstream deep into Monsal Dale. In spite of the conditions, plenty of trout were rising and a steady hatch of pale wateries suggested that a size 18 imitation would work well – and so it did. For nearly three hours I worked upstream, rising several fish in every pool or run and ending the session with seven browns and seven rainbows. The best fish, a brown of thirteen inches, was lying in a few inches of water right on the sill of Monsal Dale weir, and several times threatened to go over the fall before it was netted and released. The remainder of that day became increasingly inclement as the rain returned with renewed vigour, so I turned to the indoor attractions of Chatsworth House.

By my third and final day on the Wye the rain had moved away and once again the pale wateries emerged for two hours, this time producing eight trout, the best a fat brown of fifteen inches with large red spots and yellow sides. Then, in the evening, it was back to the sedge and blue-winged olive, with fourteen more trout before the light faded.

My second visit to the Derbyshire Wye had more than fulfilled the promise of the first trip two years earlier. I had found rising fish throughout my visit, and most of them were willing to take my imitations. In about eight hours of fishing spread over the three days I had caught and released nearly sixty trout, a strike rate for which I will always be willing to travel a long way. Even if the fishing had not been of such high quality, the opportunity to fish amid the beauty of Monsal Dale would have made the trip worth while.

23
THE TEIFI

THE TEIFI MUST be well known to most game fishermen, especially for its sea trout and salmon, but how many, I wonder, are aware of its attractions as a brown-trout stream? Unlike so many Welsh rivers, the Teifi runs most of its course through relatively lowland country, its broad, pastoral valley bounded by rounded hills rather than mountains. The result is a slower, often smooth stream, where aquatic life has more chance to become established and provide food for the trout and hatching insects to gladden the heart of an angler.

It is only in its first few miles near Llyn Teifi that the infant river can be considered a mountain stream. By the time it reaches Strata Florida it is running through meadows and then below Pontrhydfendigaid it meanders for several miles through the flatness of the strange Tregaron Bog. The cream of the trout fishing is probably from Tregaron down to Llandyssul, below which you really feel you are in the realm of the sewin and salmon.

My first-hand experience of the Teifi started only in the early eighties, but my interest in the brown-trout fishing on this Welsh stream goes back many years. I vividly recall reading an article by Oliver Kite about an early spring visit to the Teifi at Tregaron, when he fished the dark olive hatch, and created a new fly – the Imperial. Kite's evocative article convinced me that one day I must visit the Teifi and fish for its trout.

Like so many resolutions, this one slipped behind schedule and twenty years passed before I put it into practice, but in the past few years a long weekend on the Teifi has become a regular spring feature and I look forward to many more early-season visits.

AROUND TREGARON

My first visit to the Teifi was to Tregaron, when I enjoyed two days fishing the Tregaron Angling Association's lengthy stretch of water. It was late April, often a difficult time for the dry-fly angler, with the dark olives petering out and the May hatches of olive upright, pale watery and black gnat still to come. Such was the case on this occasion, with rising trout hard to find.

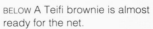

RIGHT The Teifi at Maesycrugiau: the black gnats were swarming and the trees displayed that wonderful, vivid green of spring.

BELOW A Teifi brownie is almost ready for the net.

Nevertheless, I persevered with an Imperial, in the name of tradition, on the runs below the town of Tregaron and took a fair number of hard-fighting brown trout, although none better than ten inches. Surprisingly, it was only when I fished the uppermost reaches at Strata Florida that I caught some bigger trout, including a splendid thirteen-incher that sucked in my fly in a tiny pool near the abbey.

I felt that I was really getting to grips with the Teifi trout a couple of years later, downstream at Llanfair Clydogau. I was staying at Pentre Farm, where the Davies family provides excellent accommodation with over half a mile of their own fishing as a bonus. This visit was a month later and the fly hatches were producing plenty of surface activity. During the day, hatches were fairly sparse and even the reliable black gnat was not present in its usual numbers. It was a case of walking the bank until I found a rising fish or two and then making sure that every cast earned its keep. Once, for perhaps half an hour, there was a steady stream of pale wateries coming down on the current and several trout came quickly to the net. At other times I persevered with the Black Gnat.

It was in the two evenings of my visit that the river really came to life. After dinner at the farm I hurried down across the meadow to the Teifi and was all ready to fish by half past seven. Fortunately, the temperature was holding up well in the evenings and, by the time of my arrival, spinners were already swarming over the river and the first of the trout breaking the surface. In such conditions my favourite pattern is a size 18 poly-wing Rusty Spinner, and those Teifi brownies were more than ready to take it.

Only a few yards upstream from my point of arrival a trout was in position, steadily sipping in the spinners coming down in the surface film. A quick cast and my fly was sucked in without hesitation by a lively eleven-incher, which fought well on the light tackle before being netted and returned. For the next hour the rise became increasingly frantic and a dozen trout were caught and released before quite suddenly the river went dead. Next evening, the rise lasted longer and this time over twenty trout to twelve inches were caught on the same Rusty Spinner. Unfortunately, that was the end of my fishing for that visit as the rain that had been forecast fell heavily in the night and even from the breakfast table next morning I could see that the river was in flood.

Back she goes: the Teifi near Llandyssul.

A MAY VISIT

My most recent visit to the Teifi was in May, when I enjoyed another long weekend at Pentre Farm. This visit coincided with a period of bright weather with a fresh breeze, so it was clear from the start that the fishing would not be easy. On the day of my arrival little time was left for exploring so I spent the first evening on the farm water. Predictably, the temperature dropped quickly with the approach of sunset and fly life was restricted to midges and a few olive uprights. The few fish that were rising took my size 20 Midge willingly enough but I had to settle for five trout, the best of which just made nine inches.

Next morning, I decided to explore the river downstream, thanks to Arwyn Davies's transferable ticket for the Llandyssul Anglers' Association, which has sixteen beats from Arwyn's own stretch at Llanfair Clydogau down to Newcastle Emlyn. I parked the car at Maesycrugiau, where a first look over the bridge revealed a different river from that back at Pentre Farm. Here the Teifi is much bigger, with long, deep pools, which I am sure already held some salmon and sewin. The stretch immediately above the bridge was fast and shallow, running between oak woods still showing that wonderful fresh green of spring. Already the black gnats were swarming and, although few trout were actually rising, they seemed quite willing to come up to my imitation and an hour's fishing produced eight trout to ten inches.

As I walked upstream in search of more fish, I passed a deep, slow pool where three local anglers were legering with worms on heavy tackle. With the bright sunshine and low, clear water, their prospects of catching anything were remote and I suspect that their outing was social rather than a real attempt to catch a salmon.

Half a mile upstream I found a good rise on a long, deep bend, with some of the trout throwing themselves in the air to get at the hovering black gnats. With my body waders I was able to work my way out to within easy range of the fish and pick them off one by one. By the time I stopped fishing in the early afternoon a dozen more trout had been caught and released, the best a plump trout with red spots and a yellow belly. It nudged twelve inches.

That evening, after dinner, I checked the river again, but it was even colder and the surface activity so poor that I did not bother to fish. However, nature was to provide ample compensation when Arwyn proudly showed me a pair of red kites nesting in one of the fields. As soon as we entered the field, both of these magnificent birds took to the wing and circled over us until we left. I know from experience that you can spend hours high in the nearby mountains hoping to see a kite, yet here was a pair in the gentle Teifi valley nesting on the edge of a village.

The sun was shining brightly again next morning when I went exploring even further downstream, this time driving down the long track to the river at Mackwith, near Llandyssul. Here a huge bend of the river stretching over more than half a mile offers a series of fast runs and quiet pools. The black gnat was once again the dominant fly, though a few sedges were flying over the river.

The first pool looked perfect but produced absolutely nothing, so I moved down to the next, which dropped away from a shingle beach into a long, deep stretch with a smooth unbroken surface. Several fish were rising but, with the stiff downstream breeze, covering these fish without putting them down presented a problem. I resorted to a technique that has often saved the day in such conditions – the downstream dry fly. All you have to do is aim your cast high, holding the rod back at the last moment so that the line falls slack, and then lower the rod as the fly drifts downstream. You get only a short drift but usually that is enough, and so it was on this occasion. Once again, the size 18 Black Gnat fooled those trout and the first fish was the best of the trip, a lovely fourteen-incher which made full use of the large pool before I slipped the net under him. Ten more trout were taken with the downstream technique before it was time to go.

That afternoon I had to return to Devon, but once again the Teifi had proved its worth as a brown-trout stream. So, if you are visiting the upper half of the river and can tear yourself away from the salmon and sewin, give the wild brown trout of the Teifi a try. Better still, get there in the spring, ahead of the main runs of migratory fish, when the trout fishing is probably at its best.

24

THE PIDDLE

SEVERAL YEARS AFTER I first experienced catch-and-release fishing in the United States, it came to my notice that a fishery less than two hours from home was operating on a no-kill basis. The river in question was the Piddle, a delightful little Dorset chalk stream, and the fishery was the Tolpuddle Trout Fishery, operated by Richard Slocock. Having enjoyed such splendid fishing on the other side of the Atlantic, I was eager to see if the no-kill philosophy could provide equally good results on an English chalk stream.

The Piddle rises high on the chalk downs of Dorset, a dozen miles north of Dorchester, and then runs through a lovely valley past a string of villages which take their names from the river itself – Piddletrenthide, Piddlehinton, Puddletown, Tolpuddle, Affpuddle, Briantspuddle and Turner's Puddle – before ending its course in Poole harbour.

The story goes that all of the villages were Piddles until a royal tour of the valley by Queen Victoria, when the villages which were to receive a visit quickly became Puddles, to avoid the possibility that the royal visitor might be unamused. Above Puddletown the river is very small and drops to a very low level with the arrival of summer. The best of the trout fishing is from Tolpuddle downstream, with the bottom reaches also producing small numbers of salmon and sea trout.

A NARROW STREAM

The Tolpuddle Trout Fishery is based at Lawrence's Farm and the nearest stretch of Richard Slocock's water is just across the road beyond the three small lakes which are stocked with rainbow trout. Here it is a narrow stream, in places only a couple of yards across, but broadening to possibly five yards where the two sidestreams come together. Small though it is, the Piddle here is full of fine wild brown trout. Downstream, where the river becomes considerably larger, there is another stretch of double-bank fishing at Culeaze, and upstream there is more fishing above Tolpuddle. In all, Richard Slocock offers his guests nearly four miles of the Piddle, mostly on both banks. In 1984 I called briefly at Tolpuddle to look at the fishery, but it was 1986 before I had a chance to fish it properly, when I drove to Dorset for two days of keenly anticipated fishing. My visit was on 9 and 10 June, which is normally after the mayfly, but the terrible spring of 1986, which I cursed on many occasions, really worked in my favour for once, as the mayfly hatch was still at its peak for my two days on the Piddle.

After arriving late in the morning on my first day, I spent an hour or so before lunch on the home stretch at Lawrence's Farm. It was still too early in the day for more than the odd mayfly dun, but any that appeared were quickly taken by the trout if they stayed on the river too long. Even if there were no naturals on the water, the trout were quite willing to take an artificial dropped in a likely spot, as is usually the case after the mayfly has been up for a few days.

At first the fish were quite small, mainly between eight and eleven inches, but as I moved downstream to fish the slightly wider water near the bottom of the beat some bigger fish started to show. Just at the moment when I had decided to break for lunch, a good fish moved on a bend some fifty yards above where I was fishing. By the time I was in position, the fish had stopped rising, but first cast over its lie and up it came – a plump fifteen-inch brownie which probably went a pound and a half. Even as I was playing the fish, another good trout rose to a mayfly only a yard or so upstream. The first fish was netted, unhooked and returned as quickly as possible and the fly quickly recast, with this second fish again taking without hesitation. This was a better trout, a heavily spotted cock fish, which fought powerfully before being netted and returned. It must have been all of two pounds and catching it was a good point at which to break for lunch.

CATCH AND RELEASE

Over lunch, Richard told me that the decision to go 'catch-and-release' on the Piddle had not been taken without some trepidation. Would anglers who normally expected to take away a brace or two of trout from a day on a chalk stream be willing to go home empty-handed and settle for the sport alone? Fortunately, the answer seems to be yes, which is hardly surprising as the fishing is so obviously good. Not only are there plenty of fine brown trout but there is the added pleasure of catching fish which are now predominantly stream-bred. And, if the visitor to Tolpuddle wants a few fish for the pot, there is always the opportunity to take some fish from the three stocked lakes.

After lunch, Richard took me down to Hyde, where at that time he rented nearly two miles of the lower Piddle. The top of this beat is slow and almost canal-like, backed up by a weir – ideal mayfly country. When we arrived, the afternoon hatch was already under way, with several good trout rising steadily. The first fish came readily but was only about twelve inches, but the next fish, after ignoring my mayfly several times, eventually took and proved to be a fine trout of eighteen inches, probably close to three pounds and the best fish of my visit.

In the next three hours I fished the top mile of the beat thoroughly, sticking to the wooded stretch, where the shelter from the westerly gale resulted in more mayfly and easier casting.

Ten more brownies were caught and released, with numerous fish coming adrift and one fish breaking free as it dived irresistibly for a raft of weed held back by an overhanging branch. I was using a 4lb point and really leaned on the rod, but there was no stopping this fish and the nylon broke as the trout reached cover. I hate leaving flies in fish but the barbless hook probably fell out quite soon.

Towards the end of the session, increasing numbers of spent fly came to the water and a suitable imitation worked well, although duns continued hatching well into the evening.

'After ignoring my mayfly several times...'

CLASSIC CHALK STREAM

Next day I fished the beat at Culeaze, a really classic piece of chalk stream with beds of flowering ranunculus waving in the current and the occasional rise in the clear pockets. The high wind was still with us, making casting with a big fly difficult and keeping the hatch of mayfly rather sparse. Once again, however, the trout were looking towards the surface, ready to take any well presented artificial, and fish after fish were caught and released. On this second day I had to leave by late afternoon, well before the spinner fall, so all my fish were taken on the dun.

Over the two days I had used a variety of mayfly dun imitations, with a Straddlebug style which included some orange in the hackle doing well. On one stretch, where I had difficulty keeping the fly afloat, a Humpy fly, with buoyant deer hair used for the wing, back and tail, did the trick. When spent fly were on the water I used a pattern with white abdomen, black thorax and grey squirrel tail wings, tied spent. Since then I have gone over to poly yarn for the wing, finding it much easier to use than the squirrel tail.

Apart from the obvious lure of its chalkstream trout fishing, the Piddle

ABOVE The weighted shrimp is a good standby for end-of-season days when fly hatches are sporadic. This Piddle brownie measured seventeen inches.

Mayfly time on the Piddle at Culeaze.

offers a further attraction to me as a Devon fly fisher. All of my local trout streams close on the last day of September, but the Piddle and the other Wessex rivers remain open for two more weeks until 15 October.

BACK-END BONUS

It was not until 1988 that I took advantage of this back-end bonus – to be precise, on 6 October of that year. I had telephoned Richard Slocock at Tolpuddle to see if he had a beat free and was pleased to hear that much of the water would be available. When I watched the TV weather forecast on the eve of departure my anticipation was tempered slightly by the promise of gale-force winds gusting to severe gale, with rain at first and falling temperatures. The morning drive to Dorset proved the forecast right, the car being buffeted by high winds and horizontal rain on the more open stretches, but by the time I reached Tolpuddle the clouds were beginning to break.

On arrival I tackled up and walked down to the lower beat at Tolpuddle, just beyond the lakes. Since the Piddle at Tolpuddle runs from west to east, the westerly gale was blasting downstream and there was no sign of any fly life. Even if there had been any insect activity, presenting a dry fly in the gale would have been virtually impossible, so I tied on my latest leaded pink shrimp dressing. This simple dressing was produced from some fine fur of a dull pink shade which I had acquired, and it proved to be an immediate success with both trout and grayling.

HOOK: *14 Partridge Shrimp (code K4A)*
BODY: *Dubbed pink fur started well into the bend, over an underbody of lead wire, varied according to the speed and the depth of the water*
RIB: *Fine copper wire or nylon, to prolong the life of the fly*

As soon as I saw the river, I realized that the wet weather of the 1988 summer had brought it back to a level more appropriate to early spring, an unusual sight since the Piddle normally runs very low before being replenished by the winter rains. I waded into the stream at the bottom of the beat, deciding that wading would get me not only off the skyline but also down below the worst of the gale. The fierce downstream wind still made things difficult, but the smooth shape of the shrimp sliced through it reasonably well and most of my casts ended up more or less where I wanted them. With the ruffled surface and high river, there was little chance of spotting the fish, so I concentrated on those lies which had either produced trout before or which just looked good.

FIRST CAST

My first cast was against an undercut bank on the outside of a bend and the weighted shrimp sank quickly as it drifted downstream – but not for long, as the visible part of the leader slid away almost immediately and a ten-inch brown trout was soon netted, unhooked and returned, as was an almost identical fish from virtually the same spot two casts later.

Things were looking good, especially when the next likely spot, a yard-long pocket in the weeds a short distance upstream, produced a slightly bigger trout. At this point, a few pale wateries and blue-winged olives began to emerge, but the duns were whisked away on the wind in a flash and no fish broke surface, so I stuck with the shrimp.

The Piddle at Tolpuddle splits into two streams which come together again on the beat that I was fishing, and it was just below this confluence that I encountered my next trout. This time, as I set the hook, there was a fierce pull in response and in a moment the fish was deep in weed. Handlining proved useless as the fish worked ever deeper into the subsurface greenery; then all was slack and I recovered my now shrimpless leader. Fortunately, with the river so high, the loss of that trout did not seem to have unduly disturbed the tiny stream and, only a couple of yards upstream, I was quickly into another good fish. This time all went well and a colourful cock brown of seventeen inches was netted and quickly measured before being slipped back into the river.

Just above the confluence one of the Piddle's branches runs through a small wood – and never was shelter more welcome than on that windy day. Here I caught several more fish, including another cock brown of seventeen inches, even more colourful than the first, with a yellow belly and a bright-red adipose fin. When I broke for lunch at one o'clock twelve trout had been caught and released, a satisfactory score considering the conditions.

FISH AFTER FISH

Richard Slocock was delighted when he heard of the morning's sport and when, after a lengthy lunch-time break, I moved to the upper beat for the last session, he decided to come along to watch proceedings. Above Tolpuddle, the Piddle becomes very narrow, but at the top of Richard's water there is a lovely stretch of relatively wide river for about a quarter of a mile. I slipped into the stream at the bottom of this stretch and worked upstream, with Richard watching from the bank a few yards behind. Still using the shrimp, I was immediately back in business, with fish after fish taking my pattern confidently. As I worked up two hundred yards of river in the next half-hour, nine browns to fifteen inches were netted and released, to the obvious delight of my spectator.

A year later I fished the Piddle again in October but this time I found a river that could hardly have been more different. The long dry summer of

1989 had taken its toll, and the river was reduced to a series of almost stagnant little pools. A layer of very fine silt covered the riverbed and even the movement of a trout was enough to stir it up and turn the stream muddy. A quick walk along the stream revealed plenty of fish, but making a successful approach was very difficult.

The stream was so slack that when I tried a pink shrimp it immediately sank the few inches to the bottom and lay there, so I changed to a small sinking black beetle with only a little weight.

In spite of a lot of creeping and crawling, I scared far more fish than I caught, but two good browns were eventually netted, together with a rainbow of sixteen inches. This was one of two rainbows that had been lying in full view for over a year after escaping from the lake; the other I had removed during a visit in July.

STRIPPED OF WEED

My most recent visits to the Piddle showed it in a different light and revealed another aspect of running a catch-and-release fishery. Early in 1990 heavy rain sent floods ripping down the Piddle valley and when the high levels subsided it was clear that the beat at Culeaze had been stripped of its weed, though upstream at Tolpuddle little damage was done. To the trout, and particularly wild trout, weed means food and cover and many of the fish moved out of the stretch at Culeaze, leaving only a small remaining population in the deeper pools.

In time the trout would probably have moved back naturally, but with a busy season upon him Richard Slocock decided that this was no time for purity and that some supplementary stocking was necessary on the Culeaze beat. Fortunately, with a no-kill policy these fish could be looked upon as recyclable and only about forty were introduced. Not only did these fish produce endless sport through the season of 1990 but, when I fished Culeaze twice in October, they were still there in the best of health and still very willing to take my fly. On the first visit, although little was hatching, a tiny black midge brought plenty of trout to the surface, and on my final outing it was the black bug that scored, with plenty of trout to seventeen inches. It was noticeable that as the season closed increasing numbers of wild trout were moving back into the beat.

Those visits demonstrated that running a successful catch-and-release fishery demands a degree of flexibility when extremes of weather threaten to ruin the angler's sport. Within a few weeks these stocked browns had really settled in and when I caught them late in the season I could hardly have asked for better fish.

25
THE TORRIDGE

'THE TORRIDGE', wrote Bernard Venables in his *Angler's Companion* in 1958, 'has a beauty of a special Devon kind, to enchant and still a troubled mind. In its deep valley, under the tree-hung crests, there is a seclusion as gently rurally perfect as to be found in England.'

He was writing about the Torridge as a salmon and sea-trout stream and anyone who reads the angling press will be aware of the ups and downs in the runs of migratory fish since those days. Yet, although the Torridge rightly gained its reputation for salmon and sea trout, it is also very much a brown-trout stream, which has given me countless hours of absorbing fly fishing. I would never expect to take a really big brownie on the Torridge, or make a huge catch of fish, but there are plenty of trout to be caught and enough variety of fly life to make the fishing really interesting.

The Torridge rises close to Devon's border with Cornwall, north-east of Bude, and then runs in a great loop, first in a south-easterly direction, then east before turning north until it reaches its estuary at Bideford. Throughout its length it always holds brown trout, but it is in the upper reaches, where it meanders quietly through typical North Devon farm country, that I have enjoyed most of my fly fishing for trout, at least until recently.

A HATCH OF OLIVES

Like many other anglers, my first encounter with the trout of the Torridge was on the extensive fishery of the Half Moon Inn at Sheepwash. That was on a cold, grey day back in 1976, when prospects seemed far from promising. I was fishing the stretch immediately below Sheepwash Bridge, where a series of small pools are separated by quick, broken runs, in which the wet fly that I fished all morning should have attracted the odd fish. Unfortunately, the trout stubbornly refused to show any interest until, just after noon, a few dark olive duns emerged and suddenly the river came to life as the trout eagerly seized the opportunity for some easy pickings. The transformation could hardly have been more complete, with twenty trout caught and released in the following three hours, all of them coming to a size 16 dry Kite's Imperial. All were wild fish between seven and eleven inches and most of the rises were in the quick water at the head of each pool. As the action subsided around mid-afternoon, I picked up two larger trout in the quieter water at the tail of a pool, but these were clearly freshly stocked fish that had been introduced a week or two earlier as part of the stocking carried out each year to supplement the wild trout population at Sheepwash.

Since that first visit I have fished the Torridge on many occasions, but it was in 1989 that three visits revealed the river in different moods and provided varied and challenging fishing. The first visit was on a day of bright sunshine and high temperature, so the lack of fly life came as no surprise. Fortunately there were a few black gnats hovering over the tree-lined stretch that I was fishing, about a mile below Sheepwash Bridge, and several good trout to a pound were taken on a size 18 Black Gnat during a leisurely two-hour session before I retired for refreshment in the bar at the Half Moon.

FIRST ON DRY FLY

For me, the day was memorable for the fact that my wife, Linda, took her first trout on dry fly. She had been running a wet fly through the quicker water with only a couple of pulls for reward, so I suggested a change to a dry fly and tied on a Black Gnat. The very first cast onto the smooth surface of a long pool brought an eight-inch brownie to the fly and a few seconds later it had been safely netted and returned.

A couple of weeks later, in early June, I returned to Sheepwash and this time fished the two beats above the bridge. By then the wonderful summer of 1989 was well under way and it was another brilliant day, but this time with a fresh downstream wind, which was clearly going to create problems in presenting the dry fly. Fortunately, the Torridge immediately above Sheepwash Bridge twists and turns between high banks in a way that makes it possible to avoid the worst effects of the prevailing winds. Out on the meadows the wind was quite hostile, but as I waded down in the stream the warmth of the sun created a very different environment and by mid-morning a steady flow of duns was drifting down on the stream.

This was a morning when no fly was predominant and I spent almost as much time identifying the individual species as actually fishing. First a few pale wateries emerged, followed by a trickle of olive uprights and the occasional mayfly and large brook dun. Throughout the morning there was a steady hatch of yellow may duns, easily spotted with their brilliant colour standing out against any background, but as usual the trout ignored them and stuck to the other species, which they seem to find more palatable. In such conditions a general pattern works well and in the hour before noon I took six trout to eleven inches on a size 16 hackle Adams, a great pattern when there is a variety of fly on the water.

UNDERCUT BANK

After a brief lunch back at the car, I discovered a couple of good trout rising tight against an undercut bank just above the bridge and both took the Adams without hesitation. I checked the length of each at exactly twelve inches before slipping them back.

By now the mixed hatch of the morning was dying away, but soon a few blue-winged olives began to appear and before long a really good hatch had developed. The blue-winged olive season started early on the Devon streams in 1989 and gave me some excellent daytime fishing in late May and early June on several rivers. Today was no exception and my usual daytime blue-winged olive pattern with a yellow-green body and slate-blue hackle was readily taken by any rising trout I spotted. It was never possible to settle down to fish a pool for any length of time, as only the occasional fish was rising, but those that did rise were willing takers. The key to success was to walk the bank quietly until a rise was spotted and then approach the fish carefully. Usually it took at the first cast.

Freedom regained: Torridge brown.

By the time I packed up at half past two I had caught another dozen trout to thirteen inches, but I doubt if persisting with one or two pools would have produced a quarter of that catch. In the right conditions, time spent looking for rising fish pays splendid dividends, a fact which is overlooked by so many anglers who seem prepared to stick it out in a single pool even when their perseverance is meeting with little success.

SHERRY SPINNERS

My last visit in 1989 was in the middle of July when the Torridge was rapidly diminishing to a series of still pools joined only by trickles of quicker water. This time I was to fish in the evening and, when I arrived after a day's work, Charles Inniss warned me that the going was getting tougher all the time. It was a lovely evening as I walked upstream from Sheepwash Bridge and already there were plenty of sedges flying close to the surface of the stream and soon the first sherry spinners of the evening began to return to the water. In such conditions I usually start with a small Sedge and then change to a Sherry Spinner, but right from the start it was the Sherry Spinner that the fish wanted that evening, even though the sedges were more numerous.

The bright sun shining straight downstream was quite a problem as it dropped towards the horizon, but once it had set I was able to fish into the afterglow until it was virtually dark. In the dying orange light the characteristic sipping rises of the trout as they took the spinners could be easily spotted and most of the fifteen trout that I hooked came after sunset. The majority of the fish were between seven and ten inches, with only one reaching eleven inches, but such a catch was very welcome in the drought conditions.

WONDERFUL SECLUSION

The lower and middle reaches of rivers best known for their salmon and sea-trout fishing often offer mile after mile of water which is hardly touched by the trout fishermen, yet in many cases they are missing some of the best fly fishing on the river. Such stretches can hold plenty of trout of good average size and they will often be truly wild, as there is little incentive for stocking where most anglers are seeking salmon or sea trout. Such is the case on the Torridge, where the middle and lower river meanders through a lovely wooded valley, so secluded that to reach the river it is often necessary to drive down a mile of track and then walk some distance to the stream. Once you have reached the river, I know of few places which offer more peace or a greater sense of being away from the outside world. The part of the river upstream of Great Torrington as far as Meeth offers wonderful seclusion, and it was on the Little Warham fishery that I fished it for the first time in 1990.

It was the afternoon of the Spring Bank Holiday Monday, a time when any stream with public access or near the road is hardly worth fishing, but at Little Warham all was peace and I never saw another person throughout the afternoon. At first glance, when I arrived at two o'clock, conditions looked far from ideal, with brilliant sunshine beating down on a skeletal river, as the 1990 drought was already well established by late May. Fast-flowing shallow water seemed the best bet in the conditions, so I headed upstream towards a broken stretch which I could just see from the elderly fishing hut where I reached the river bank. As I walked past the smooth slower-flowing stretch

A one pound trout safely in the net on the Little Warham Fishery on the Torridge

above the hut, there was no sign of rising trout, even though some sedges, black gnats and the occasional mayfly could be seen, and when I arrived at the quicker water it seemed at first glance to be equally barren.

BROKEN WATER

I tied on a size 16 Hairwing Sedge, always a good bet for fishing over broken water on a sunny day, and there were enough natural sedges on the wing to back that choice. As I waded out into the knee-deep water I saw my first rise, and then several more, all in equally shallow water close to the edge of the trees along the far bank. But they were all tiny rises and at first I was reluctant to cast to them since they were probably made by fish of only five or six inches. But nothing else was on offer so eventually I cast to the closest rise, the sedge was sucked in and I found myself playing a trout of ten inches. Several more fish came from the same shallow stretch, the best just short of a foot in length, proof that we can all be deceived by the appearance of a rise.

As the afternoon progressed a few blue-winged olives began to emerge and I became aware of some surface activity downstream in the deeper water. A short walk revealed several trout sucking in the blue-winged olive duns and this time the rise forms suggested fish of a fair size. The first fish refused my blue-winged olive imitation at least a dozen times and then took it after a cast that appeared no different from those that had gone before. It was a brightly coloured wild fish which fought hard before being netted, quickly measured and then slipped back into the river. The tape measure said 14½ inches and it would probably have weighed a good pound. Two more fish were hooked and lost in quick succession and then another was netted, this time just on fourteen inches. The successful fly had been a size 16 Comparadun with the yellow-olive body that usually works well when blue-winged olives hatch in the day.

26
THE TAMAR

*L*EARNING HOW TO catch wild trout on a small stream can be a frustrating business, but over the years countless budding anglers must have taken the short cut to success and caught their first fish during a fly-fishing course at the Arundell Arms in the far west of Devon. There the River Tamar is fed by half a dozen tributaries – Lyd, Carey, Wolf, Thrushel, Lew and Ottery – and it is to these little streams that meander along their deep-cut courses among the meadows that I frequently return for their wild and often prolific brown trout. With some twenty miles of water controlled by the hotel, there is a wonderful variety of fishing to choose from. Indeed, the choice can be daunting but bailiffs Roy Buckingham and David Pilkington are normally on hand to advise where to go and how to fish.

At a casual glance, these little streams are hardly impressive. Usually they have cut a deep channel in the soft soil, often running five or six feet below the meadows with sheer banks, and with the exception of the Lyd, which comes down from Dartmoor, they never run really clear. So, what is the attraction of these modest and rather coloured little streams?

Perhaps their greatest charm is their intimacy. Everything is on a small scale and there is never any chance of being overawed by these little brooks. Even the beginner can quickly spot the places where the trout are likely to be – the quick narrow throat at the head of a pool, the numerous undercut banks where the trout lie within inches of the eroded clay, or an eddy beneath an overhanging tree. When few fish are rising, you always fish with hope when a stream advertises its secrets so freely.

And then there are the trout themselves, usually from eight to ten inches but with plenty of foot-long fish. A few fish are stocked each year, especially on the beats near the hotel where they give the novice a sporting chance of catching a reasonable fish, but mostly they are wild. Indeed, for many years the hotel policy has been to encourage anglers to practise catch-and-release with barbless hooks so that the wild stocks can be maintained.

LEFT Keeping low and casting a dry fly to the far side of the Carey. The trout sometimes lie within inches of the steep bank.

BELOW Wet fly on the Quarry Pool, part of the Arundell Arms' Tamar water.

MAYFLY LARVAE

The mud that washes in from the surrounding farmland and accumulates wherever the flow is slack provides the habitat liked by mayfly larvae and my first encounter with these western brooks was at mayfly time. I had been allocated a beat on the Carey and, although the short mayfly season was well advanced, there were still enough duns and spinners on the water to keep the trout interested. I was introducing a relative newcomer to stream fishing that day and even he had no difficulty in catching a few fish.

On most beats at the Arundell Arms a degree of bank clearing is carried out and there are stiles to get you from field to field. Beat 5 on the Thrushel, however, is allowed to go its own way and at first glance much of it looks like an unfishable jungle. The banks are high and the bankside growth often makes access to the stream impossible over lengthy stretches. The only answer is to use a short rod, don a pair of full-length waders, get into the water where it joins the Wolf, and fish upstream without ever leaving the stream.

Even then it can be tough going, but the results can be dramatic, as I discovered one day in the mayfly season a few years ago. I had driven down to Lifton through heavy rain, which fortunately cleared around mid-morning, and I made a start on the Carey at half past eleven. There was no fly on the water and not a sign of a rise, but David Pilkington had told me that there had been hatches of mayfly so that was what I tied on. An hour's fishing proved that the trout were still looking for the mayfly and six were caught, but not one exceeded eight inches and the better fish seemed completely absent.

Soon after 12.30 I checked back at the hotel and was told that Beat 5 on the Thrushel was free and invited to give it a try. Even as I waded into the bottom pool of the beat it was clear that here the fish were really active, with five or six rising in that one pool. Two fish came quickly to the pink mayfly that I had tied on and then a better trout rose several times right under the bole of an old ash tree at the head of the pool. At the second attempt the fly dropped right against the tree and a moment later I was playing a trout that proved to be the best of the day, a thirteen-incher with bright red spots, yellow belly and white leading edges on its fins.

A TWITCHED FLY

In the next pool, nothing was rising and when I dropped my fly on the water it was at first ignored. Then I gave it a twitch and immediately it was taken. And so it continued, with every pool producing at least a brace of trout. In those pools with rising trout I fished the fly with a dead drift, and on those where nothing stirred I resorted to twitching the fly – and the trout just kept coming whichever method was used. Beat 5 is a lengthy stretch of water, well over a mile, and it was 5.30 by the time I reached the top of the beat, but by then my tally of trout caught and returned had topped eighty, a tribute to the head of fish in this secluded little stream.

Although most of my fishing on the Tamar tributaries has been with the dry fly, these streams respond very well to the wet fly and nymph. David Pilkington is a great advocate of the wet fly, which he fishes up and across, and retrieves slightly faster than the current, and I have seen him put this technique to very good use. His favourite wet flies are the Coachman and Pilk's Favourite, a sort of wet Rough Olive.

A few years ago the Arundell Arms acquired some new water on the Ottery, which runs in from Cornwall, and it was there that I enjoyed success with a nymph in miserable conditions. It was raining when I arrived, continued raining and, if anything, was raining more heavily when I departed. There was no sign of fly and even if a fish had moved it would have been impossible to see it in the rain-lashed surface. The nymph seemed the only possibility so on went a size 14 weighted Pheasant Tail Nymph. Some of the pools on the Ottery are very deep, but the nymph sank quickly in the slow water and the trout responded well when it was activated by a lift of the rod, especially when the nymph was allowed to run down the current close to a sheer clay bank. The couple of hours up to noon produced eight trout to ten inches, which were very welcome on an unpromising morning.

27

PENNSYLVANIA LIMESTONE

*L*ONG BEFORE I ever fished in the State of Pennsylvania, I felt that I knew its rivers and trout almost as well as those in England. Over many discussions with Sid Neff in Ireland and England, and in correspondence after his return to the United States after his sojourn in Ireland, he had told me of the many trout streams that he fished in his home state, particularly those that spring from the limestone and provide fishing akin to that of our chalk streams. He had told me of the Letort and Falling Springs Run and Spruce Creek and other streams that had put Pennsylvania and its fly fishers right at the forefront of American dry-fly fishing. I had also learned about anglers and writers such as Vince Marinaro and Charlie Fox, who had fished those streams through good times and bad times, and created methods and fly patterns that would deceive those contemptuous trout, and had proved effective on waters in many countries.

The natural trout in Pennsylvania is not a trout at all but a char – the so-called brook trout, *Salvelinus fontinalis*. This is a beautiful fish much cherished by American anglers as a vital piece of their angling heritage, but it has to be admitted that it is not ideally suited to the modern age. It demands cool water, which has gradually been reduced through deforestation and industry, and its readiness to take the angler's lure quickly led to many rivers being fished out. Today it is the rainbow trout and, in particular, the brown trout that form the basis of Pennsylvania trout fishing. The rainbow, which can be reared to catchable size at low cost, is the mainstay on stocked rivers, with the brown predominant on those streams which are loved by the dedicated fly fisher.

Although Pennsylvania has many good freestone streams, as Americans call their rain-fed rivers, it is the streams that issue from the bed of limestone in the centre of the state that give it its fame among trout fishermen. Until 1977 I had only been able to imagine this fishing, but then I at last set aside the time and the money to make a fishing trip in the autumn of that year and sample American fishing for the first time.

It was also to be my first opportunity to sample catch-and-release fisheries, which I had read much about in American magazines and often

ABOVE Falling Springs Run: a
beautiful limestone stream in
Pennsylvania.

LEFT A Letort brown is slipped
back among the watercress
beds.

discussed with Sid. The Fish and Game Commission in Pennsylvania was one of the first to set aside stretches of river where only the fly could be used and all trout had to be returned immediately to the stream. As in so many of the more heavily populated states, many lovely streams had become little more than put-and-take fisheries, with frequent stocking with takable trout. Gradually, however, pressure from serious trout fishermen had convinced them that there was a better way and no-kill signs began to appear on stretches of river capable of maintaining a wild trout population.

In mid-September I flew into Pittsburgh and spent two days with Sid Neff and his wife at their home in Sewickley, north of the city. During that time we made our final preparations for a trip that would be split between trout fishing in Pennsylvania and a quest for land-locked salmon in Maine. On one of our visits to downtown Pittsburgh I called at Allegheny County Hall to get my non-resident licence while Sid made last-minute arrangements for his graphic design business to mark time for a couple of weeks. Then we were off.

FALLING SPRINGS

Our first destination was Falling Springs Run, a small stream near the town of Chambersburg in central Pennsylvania. This is limestone country and the river bore an extraordinary resemblance to a minor English chalk stream, about the size of the Lambourn. It was late September, a time when most of the major fly hatches were over for the year, but we were hoping that the tiny *Tricorythodes* would still be active. When we made a start at the top of the fishery soon after breakfast, however, the only flies to be seen were tiny midges hovering in the cool air. A few were falling on the stream and several fish were sipping on a smooth straight stretch above a small artificial weir. We spent an hour working over those fish with size 22 Grey Midges and fine leader points and, although some were put down, we succeeded in catching several trout each. They proved to be rainbows of modest size, with nothing in excess of ten inches.

As the morning progressed, we moved downstream, and with no evidence of insect activity we tied on little black deer-hair beetles in the hope that the trout might be looking for any terrestrials that might find their way onto the stream. The few rising fish that we found came willingly to the beetle, and now they were all browns. By lunch time Sid had taken the best fish, a fourteen-incher.

By early afternoon we became aware of large balls of insects hovering over the river, and Sid told me that these were the *Tricorythodes* spinners that we had been hoping for. Eventually they broke up and fell upon the stream, bringing about a startling transformation. The previously quiet stream suddenly boiled with trout eagerly feeding on the spinners and we quickly tied on size 20 imitations, very similar to our own tiny caenis. I was standing on the inside of a bend and within easy casting range there must have been more than twenty trout rising steadily, and fifty yards upstream Sid was confronted by a similar sight.

I soon learned that the comparison I had made between the *Tricorythodes* and the caenis extended to the fishing too. Many of us have experienced huge hatches of caenis, with trout rising everywhere but almost impossible to catch. Those trout on Falling Springs Run were just as difficult, probably due to the huge numbers of natural insects, but the sheer quantity of fish in a small area made it possible to catch a few. By the time the rise petered out, we had taken a dozen browns between us, but we both realized that we had failed to capitalize on the full potential of that extraordinary rise. The stretch we were fishing was strictly catch-and-release and the prolific head of fish on such a heavily fished water was proof of the success of the management policy.

Rules and regs: Falling Springs.

THE LETORT

The next day was spent on the Letort, probably Pennsylvania's most famous trout stream, where Vince Marinaro did much of the fishing that inspired his *Modern Dry Fly Code*. The Letort was quite unlike any other river I had ever seen, with its smooth currents sliding past huge beds of watercress, some of it so thick that it was possible to walk on it without breaking through. One glance at the silky surface of the stream left no doubt why this river had gained such a reputation for its sophisticated trout – the slightest imperfection in presentation would be painfully obvious.

The lack of any fly, except a few of the bright yellow sulphur duns, immediately made it clear that we would have to go seeking the brown trout of the Letort. Sid had told me that a prime source of trout food was the cress bug, a waterlouse that flourished in the cress beds, and that I should look out for the tails of fish that were searching for food. We were using simple size 14 imitations with cigar-shaped bodies of natural sheep's wool and plenty of lead to get the fly down quickly – rather similar to Sawyer's Killer Bug.

Much of the Letort is deep with a soft bottom, so as there was no question of wading we walked up the bank in search of our first fish. When Sid spotted a waving tail against the watercress on the far side of the stream, he generously offered me the first chance and I dropped the Cress Bug into the stream just short of the weeds. It sank and when the leader slid away a quick strike hooked my first Letort trout. Unfortunately, its first rush took it deep into the cress and we parted company, but when I hooked the next fish, some fifty yards upstream, I applied maximum pressure immediately and hauled the fish away from the weeds. In the open water it was soon under control and I netted a heavily spotted fifteen-inch brown.

As we worked our way up the river the odd fish was rising and, in the absence of any hatching fly, we tackled them with dry terrestrial patterns. Sid was using a Hopper, to suggest the grasshoppers and crickets that were so numerous in the riverside meadows, and I was using a black Deerhair Beetle, and both of us took fish from the top on these patterns. We failed to take any of the very big fish for which the Letort was renowned, but Sid's best brown went sixteen inches and we each had several fish only just short of that size.

On both the Letort and Falling Springs Run there was always the feeling that suburbia was encroaching just over the horizon, though the rivers and their surrounding meadows still had a fragile beauty. In a well populated area with a lot of trout fishermen, there was no doubt that the quality fishing that we enjoyed could only have been maintained by the no-kill policy in operation on these streams.

After leaving the Letort, we headed north-east for a week of fishing for landlocked salmon, but on our way back we fished once more for Pennsylvania trout in the last few days of the season. Then we caught a mixture of browns, rainbows and brook trout on a variety of streams. At Big Spring Creek we fished within a few yards of the huge spring that produced an instant trout stream thirty feet wide; on the exclusive Rolling Rock estate with its manicured stream we enjoyed easy pickings with freshly stocked trout; and at Spruce Creek we sampled one of the best club fisheries in Pennsylvania.

My introduction to American fishing had given me only a small sample of the trout streams of Pennsylvania, but it was enough to show why those limpid limestone streams have such an important place in the American fly-fishing heritage.

28
THE ROCKY MOUNTAINS

*B*Y A FORTUNATE dispensation of nature, perhaps with a little help from man, there are on this planet a few places where, in a relatively small area, the fly fisher can enjoy trout fishing of a quality and variety that a visitor from less favoured areas finds difficult to believe. From this short and select list, one of the best is that part of the western United States of America where the states of Montana, Wyoming and Idaho meet. Here, an area little more than a hundred miles across offers a bewildering range of streams, from the little spring creeks that could be Wessex chalk streams but for the backdrop of mountains to big roaring rivers like the Madison.

Anyone who has a passing knowledge of the trout streams of the world will have read of these streams – the Yellowstone, Firehole, Madison, Bighole, Snake, and many others. I too had read of these streams, their beautiful surroundings, prolific fly hatches and splendid trout, and then a few years ago I decided that the time had come to see if the fishing was as good as the press notices suggested.

My old friend, Sid Neff, from Pittsburgh, informed me that he could get away for a three-week trip so we planned our visit for late June and early July, just at the end of spring in the high country of the Rockies. From Pittsburgh we flew west via Chicago, Denver and Salt Lake City to Bozeman in Montana, the jumping-off point for our trip. There we collected a rented station wagon and headed east to Livingston, where we picked up our licences at Dan Bailey's Fly Shop and got the latest information from George Anderson, who was then still working at Bailey's before setting up his own tackle and guiding operation. He told us that the Firehole in Yellowstone National Park was fishing well, but first we were to enjoy an afternoon of easy fishing on Armstrong Spring Creek to get us started.

Armstrong is a short crystal-clear limestone stream which bubbles up from a huge spring and runs its short course down to the Yellowstone River. It is famous for its chalkstream-type fishing. We parked the car by DePuys Ranch right by the stream, bought our permits from the rancher, and set off in search of my first Rocky Mountain trout. On that bright June afternoon with a hot wind there was never to be any sign of hatching flies but the stream was full of rainbow trout which were eager to grab a sunk fly.

At first we took fish on a small black nymph and, following a suggestion made by George Anderson, I tied on a Woolly Bugger. I felt rather guilty about using such a creation on a limestone stream, but George had said that if nothing was moving it would deliver the goods if cast upstream and brought back a little quicker than the current. How right he was! As I worked up the shallow water in front of the ranch house, fish after fish came bow-waving at the fly, taking it savagely in a way that seemed quite inappropriate to the water that I was fishing. When we packed up to head south for Yellowstone, Sid and I had caught twenty-five rainbows apiece, with the best fish about two pounds, and we felt that our holiday had really started.

THE FIREHOLE

After overnighting in West Yellowstone, we entered the park gates, making sure that we had the fishing permits that are included in the park entry fee, and headed up the Madison River and then up the Firehole. The Firehole has often been called the strangest trout stream on earth, and you quickly realize why. As you drive up the river you soon see the steam rising from one of the areas of thermal activity, where geysers, steam vents and hot springs give the area its unique flavour. And in the midst of this primeval activity flows the smooth Firehole river, with its level banks, gravel bottom, huge hatches of small flies and its trout, a mix of browns and rainbows. The rules are quite simple – fly only and a limit of two trout of not less than sixteen inches.

Our destination was Biscuit Basin, only two miles downstream from Old Faithful, the most famous geyser in the park. A half-mile walk downstream from the car park took us to a lovely broad stretch of the river where already the first few fish were rising. As anticipated, the hatching insects were pale morning duns (*Ephemerella enermis* and *infrequens*), a member of the same genus as our blue-winged olive which is both common and widespread in the West. I had already tied some hackle patterns, with yellow-olive body and light olive hackle on a 16 hook, while Sid was using a Comparadun with similar colour scheme.

Fortunately, our walk had taken us well beyond the sightseers around the car park and we were able to settle down to stalking the rising trout without disturbance. Sid started by casting from the bank on a stretch that was too deep to wade and, although the swirling current made it difficult to avoid drag, he quickly took two rainbows of about a pound. I moved off downstream to a broad stretch which appeared devoid of rising trout, but when I took a closer look I could just see a line of rises right against the undercut bank thirty yards away. By wading carefully twenty yards across the stream I was able to drop my fly tight against the bank, right where the trout were rising. Three hard-fighting rainbows were safely netted and released, and then a better fish sucked in the fly and rushed downstream. That smooth-looking current was deceptively fast and there was no hope of bringing the fish back upstream on the fine leader, so I had no choice but to wade ashore, walk downstream of the fish and eventually net an eighteen-inch brown in quieter water. Several times in the next couple of days Sid and I would have to use similar tactics to net good fish.

For the remainder of that day and the next morning, in brilliant sunny weather, it was the pale morning duns that the trout wanted, but the second afternoon had a surprise in store for us. We suddenly realized that the sky was darkening, the temperature was dropping and soon a fierce wind was blowing across the valley. We were about to pack up when we realized that huge numbers of tiny flies were hatching and trout were rising everywhere.

Leaving the water with such a rise in full swing would have been out of the question, so we braved the weather, changed our flies and went back to it. The hatching flies were *Pseudocloëon* and the best imitation in my box was a size 20 Pale Watery. Although it was rather larger than the naturals, the trout did not seem to mind. At times the rises were so frequent that it was difficult to know if the trout had taken a natural or the imitation, but striking every time that a fish rose near where we thought our fly was drifting kept us busy playing fish. Eventually our flies became sodden and bedraggled, and it was only when we tried to tie on new flies that we realized how far the temperature had dropped. Our hands were so numb that it was impossible to bring finger and thumb together, so it was back to the car and the comfort of the heater. Next morning there was three inches of snow on the ground, but by noon it had all gone, the sun was out, the temperature in the seventies, and the pale morning duns were hatching again.

Madison rainbow on the Montana.

THE MADISON

Our next river could not have been more different. For a change we drove west from West Yellowstone to the Madison, a big fast-flowing stream which has been described as one long riffle throughout its length. Indeed, at first glance it is difficult to see where the fish can find any shelter from the current, but there is no doubt that the Madison has a huge population of browns and rainbows, some of them very big fish. The strength of the stream really becomes apparent the moment you step into it, with the force of the

LEFT The sheer vastness of Henry's Fork is daunting at first sight.

BELOW The Firehole: where geysers, steam vents and hot springs give this trout river a most unusual quality.

current making a wading staff essential even when you are little more than ankle-deep, so if you are at all apprehensive about wading the Madison is not for you.

Nor is this a water for light rods, long leaders and tiny flies. The main food item is the huge stonefly, *Pteronarchys californica*, both in the nymph form and when it hatches into the so-called salmon fly, which is imitated by the aptly named dry fly the Sofa Pillow. Our visit was ahead of the salmon fly hatch so we would be using a pattern to suggest the nymph, and we had already tied up plenty of well weighted Montana Nymphs on size 6 extra-long-shank hooks. Yes, the Montana Nymph, which has become one of the most widely used general patterns on stillwaters in Britain, was originally designed to suggest the big western stonefly. Our nymphs were tied onto short leaders with 6 lb breaking strain points, with fast sinking No. 7 lines and matching nine-foot rods.

Our starting point was at the first bridge below Quake Lake, which was created by an earthquake in 1959 when 80 million tons of rock and earth slid into the valley to form a dam. The river was running fast and clear, thanks to the settling effect of Quake Lake and Hebgen Lake upstream, at a time when most of the freestone rivers were coloured from the spring run-off. The combination of broken water sparkling in the morning sunshine and the backdrop of snow-topped mountains sharpened our anticipation as we approached the river, and the Fish and Game Commission notice that stated fly-only and no-kill gave the confidence that comes from knowing that the river has not been cleaned out by fishmongers.

It was clear right from the start that the river was full of fish, a mix of browns and rainbows with the odd whitefish taking our nymphs from virtually the first cast. The trick was to spot a pocket in the current created by underwater boulders and then cast upstream so that the sinking line and weighted fly were down deep by the time the fly reached the pocket. Hooking the fish was no problem, as the trout had to grab any food passing in the fast current or it gone for ever, so most takes were fast and solid with the fish often hooking itself. Even with the strong tackle, those trout had to be played carefully as they ran, bored and jumped in the fast water, and many of them were in the sixteen-to-eighteen-inch class.

HENRY'S FORK

After spending four days based at West Yellowstone, we drove to Last Chance, Idaho, to fish Henry's Fork on the Snake River, and in particular the superb water running through the Harriman Ranch, a state park. This wonderful piece of water looks like a huge chalk stream that has been created for the fly fisher, running from knee- to waist-deep over smooth gravel and varying from 200 to 400 feet wide. In fact, the even flow is controlled by Island Park Reservoir, a few miles upstream.

As on the Firehole, the fishing through the morning and early afternoon was dominated by the *Ephemerella* species, but with greater variety. In addition to the pale morning duns, there were hatches of the western green drake (*Ephemerella grandis*) and the brown drake (*Ephemerella simulans*), and, when we had the energy to fish the evenings, there were huge hatches of very small caddis. The rules allowed anglers to keep as many fish as they liked under twelve inches and one fish over twenty inches, but nothing in between, but in practice I never saw a fish kept, though many were caught in our four days on Henry's Fork.

With the exception of a few small brook trout, all of the fish that we caught were rainbows, and undoubtedly the most difficult and educated rainbows that I have ever encountered, which was hardly surprising on a heavily fished river where countless fish are caught and returned. Fortunately, the river is so big that it can absorb large numbers of anglers and the rising fish so numerous that plenty were caught even though many refused our best efforts. I worked over one rainbow of about three pounds for half an hour and, although it came up and looked at every new fly that I tried, it never took but each time returned to feeding steadily on naturals. Sid took over for half an hour with equal lack of success, so whoever said that a trout that keeps rising will make a mistake sooner or later had definitely not met this fish.

Around noon on the second day there was a good hatch of western green drakes and the opportunity to use a bigger fly, almost as big as our own mayfly, made the fishing just that little bit easier. Our target was a twenty-inch rainbow but, although we had fish after fish over nineteen inches, it was not until the third evening that I took a genuine twenty-incher in a huge hatch of caddis, using a size 18 Hairwing. On the fourth and final day, George Anderson drove down from Livingston to join us, and showed us how it was done by taking a big rainbow lying against the bank that we had both failed to lure. Even George, with his many years of local experience, needed four changes of fly to fool it but eventually he took a flawless rainbow of twenty-one inches on a Pale Morning Dun Emerger.

Sadly, the news from Henry's Fork in the last few years has not been good, with reports of a lack of big fish – possibly because of insufficient releases of water from Island Park Reservoir in the winter and low flows resulting in fish kills in the harsh winter weather.

During the rest of our trip we fished Sixteen Mile Creek, where I took my first cutthroat trout, and Benhart's Spring Creek, a dry-fly stream near Bozeman. We finished up with a wonderful Sunday afternoon when George Anderson took us to Nelson's Spring Creek. This exquisite little limestone stream, beneath the snow-capped peaks of the Absaroka Range, was teeming with free-rising rainbows and our final afternoon produced nearly thirty trout apiece. In seventeen days we had enjoyed superby fly fishing and caught nearly five hundred fish, but had still only skimmed the surface of the wealth of trout fishing in that part of the Rocky Mountains.

29
IN THE
KERRY MOUNTAINS

BY ANY STANDARDS, Kerry in the south-west of Ireland is a county of extraordinary natural beauty, and its magnificent mountains and coast can be seen at their best from the famous Ring of Kerry. The problem is that, at times, the Ring can be too popular for its own good, with tourists' cars and coaches trailing from one beauty spot to the next, and increasing numbers of undistinguished bungalows sprawling out from the towns and villages. But if you take to the side roads, park your car and set off on foot into the wild country that starts within yards of the tourist route, you will quickly discover mountain streams and loughs that are home to some of the wildest and most colourful trout you are ever likely to find.

This is not a place for anyone seeking big trout; indeed, Kerry trout could be described as definitely on the small side. But they are truly wild, incredibly prolific on some waters and often very easy to catch, and much of the fishing is absolutely free. What this adds up to is an area ideal for casual fishing and for beginners. You can drive along admiring the scenery and stop to fish several loughs or streams in the course of a day, with every chance of catching several dozen brown trout of modest size.

WILD WATERS

I first discovered the wild waters of Kerry more than twenty years ago and then, in 1990, returned with my wife to enjoy three days of productive but undemanding fly fishing. From my original visit I remembered well the string of small lakes in the Gap of Dunloe, the beauty spot in the shadow of McGillycuddy's Reeks, Ireland's highest mountains. Then the lakes had been full of eager little browns and I wondered if anything had changed in a couple of decades, so it was in the Gap that we made a start.

We arrived at the car park opposite Kate Kearney's Cottage, at the foot of the Gap, at around noon on a day of brilliant sunshine. Already tourists from all over the world were gathering but, in early June, their numbers were still quite small and they were easily left behind once we started up the track into the Gap. A half-mile walk brought us to Black Lake, the first of the series, and on its banks I put the rods together, threaded the lines and tied on

ABOVE Linda Weaver fishes the
rocky stream between the two
loughs at Cummeenduff Glen.

RIGHT Small but beautiful: a
brownie from the Gap of
Dunloe still shows the 'finger-
marks' characteristic of the
parr.

size 14 Bibios, one with a red centre and the other green. To get things started, I set up Linda's outfit first and even as I turned to organize my own outfit she was into a small trout with her first cast. Indeed, she had caught and returned four and missed several more before I had made a cast.

That first cast produced an offer, as did the next ten, with some trout caught and returned, some missed at the take and others coming adrift while being played. All were brilliantly coloured, with yellow bellies, bright-red spots, white-edged anal and ventral fins, and red rims round their tails. Most of the fish were between six and eight inches, with the occasional monster nudging nine inches. After ten or a dozen fish each from one spot, the rises to our flies would slow down, but it only needed a move of a few yards along the lake shore and the sport would start all over again.

We were both fishing with 8½-foot carbon rods, WF5F lines and single flies tied to leader points of about 3lb breaking strain. Although we were using wet flies, many fish took as the fly hit the water and only occasionally did a fly sink sufficiently for the take not to be a visible rise or boil.

The next day was dull, wet and windy, with little opportunity to fish, but by the following morning the bright weather had returned and we headed for Moll's Gap on the Killarney–Kenmare road, and turned onto the minor road that leads to the valleys above the Lakes of Killarney. My first cast of the day was on the tumbling Owenreagh River, still on the high side after the previous day's rain, and then I moved on to the Gearhameen River. Both streams were full of free-taking trout which came readily to the Bibio that I had used for lake fishing, and plenty of fish up to nine or ten inches were caught and released. Perhaps because of the high water, the wet fly worked best and, although I tried a dry fly for a while, the trout showed little interest in the floater.

DEEP IN THE MOUNTAINS

Then we headed into Cummeenduff Glen, a lovely and remote spot deep in the mountains, with two medium-sized lakes. Before starting to fish, we checked at the farm that it was in order to fish, and the farmer and his wife gave us the go-ahead. In fact, the farmer told us that he had a boat on the upper lake and that I was welcome to use it, a typical reaction from the hospitable Irish.

In spite of the remoteness, a reasonably smooth track gives access to both lakes and we parked overlooking the point where a little stream leaves the upper lake and runs its short course of about 200 yards to the lower lake. On our arrival both lakes were flat calm, so we fished the little stream and found it full of tiny trout. Then a breeze sprang up briefly and I managed one good drift in the boat. A few fish had started to show on the lake and the same Bibio must have risen twenty-five fish during the drift, but only five of them stuck, all trout of eight or nine inches.

Later that day, as we headed for Killarney, we parked beside the main road and walked the few yards to the bank of Looscaunagh Lough. This is a narrow lake nearly a mile long, with easy banks and absolutely bursting with small trout. Once again we were into fish right away and, as we fished along a quarter of a mile of bank, we caught and released dozens of small trout. This really was the ideal place for the beginner to practise the basic skills of fishing – casting, striking, hooking, unhooking, and so on. And the fly? The Bibio, of course!

The following morning I had one last chance for an hour's fishing before heading east, and chose the River Flesk at Clonkeen on the main road that heads east from Killarney towards Cork. The river here, with its smooth gravel bed, was ideal for wading, even though it was still running fast after the rain of two days earlier. The river was dropping fast, but still carrying peat stain, so I tied on a couple of size 14 wet flies – a Grizzle Palmer on the point and a Rough Olive on the dropper.

There were plenty of fish in the heads of the pools, very willing to take my flies, but all were tiny trout or salmon parr and it was only when I had waded down to the middle of each pool that I began to pick up better fish, with the best fish coming from the quiet smooth water towards the tail of each pool.

FREE FISHING

Although so much of the trout fishing in Kerry is absolutely free, there are waters which are strictly preserved, so you need to know in advance where you can and cannot fish. When I first visited Kerry, I planned my visit with the help of *Brown Trout Fishing in Ireland*, a splendid little booklet compiled by the Inland Fisheries Trust and published by the Irish Tourist Board in 1967. Not only did this booklet tell me where I could fish; it also gave guidance on the quality of each lough or stream. Although my ageing copy of *Brown Trout Fishing in Ireland* proved equally useful in 1990, it has long been out of print and a copy would probably be very difficult to find. Fortunately, the well-known authority on Irish fishing, Peter O'Reilly, has written *Trout and Salmon Loughs of Ireland*, which was published in 1987, and is essential reading for anyone planning a fishing trip to Ireland. Now, he has written a splendid companion volume entitled *Trout and Salmon Rivers of Ireland – An Angler's Guide* (1991).

Whatever has changed in Ireland, the far south-west continues to provide that rare commodity, free fishing for genuinely wild trout, and I hope it continues to do so for a long time. While it does, I can think of few better places to introduce a novice to the pleasures of fly fishing for wild brown trout – and there are times when even the most experienced angler enjoys some easy pickings.

WHERE TO FIND THE FISH

V IRTUALLY ALL OF the waters described in this book could be fished by any visitor and, in spite of the fact that fisheries inevitably change ownership, most if not all of them still can. In some cases you have to stay at a hotel to gain access, but most of these waters can be fished simply by purchasing a licence or a permit.

Here, then, is a list of fisheries from which I have derived great pleasure over the years – some on a regular basis and others on all too rare visits. Details are also given for some other fisheries nearby, for which permits can be obtained.

USK
Permits for the Usk Town Water from Sweet's Tackle Shop, Usk, Gwent.

SUIR
Permits for Thurles, Holycross and Ballycamas Anglers' Association waters from O'Gorman's Bar, Bohernacrusha and Hayes Hotel, Thurles. The waters of the Cashel, Golden and Tipperary Angling Club, which I have not fished, are only a few miles downstream: permits from J. Ryan, Friar Street, Cashel, and G. Hogan, Golden Village.

UPPER DART
Permits for Duchy of Cornwall waters from many shops, post offices and inns in and around Dartmoor.

UPPER TEIGN
Permits for Upper Teign Fishing Association waters from Angler's Rest at Fingle Bridge, Drewsteignton, Devon, and other agents in the area.

CULM
The fishery described is owned by the Metters family and day permits can sometimes be obtained by telephoning Craddock 40205.

OTTER
Fishing available at Deer Park Hotel, Buckerell village, near Honiton, Devon.

EXE AND TRIBUTARIES

Unfortunately the Tiverton Fly Fishers' Club restricts membership to residents in the old Borough of Tiverton, and no day permits are issued. On the Barle, fishing is available at the Tarr Steps Hotel, Hawkridge, Dulverton, Somerset. The Carnarvon Arms Hotel, Dulverton, has fishing on the Exe and Barle. Permits for the Exe and Haddeo are available from John Sharpe, Parlour Cottage, Higher Grants Farm, Exebridge, Dulverton, Somerset.

LYN

The Watersmeet and Glenthorne Fisheries on the East Lyn are managed by the National Rivers Authority and permits can be purchased at local agents.

DERBYSHIRE WYE

The fishing in and around Monsal Dale is part of the Chatsworth Estate and permits for the upper part of the fishery can be obtained from the Estate Office at Edensor near Bakewell. The whole of the fishery is available to guests at the Cavendish Hotel at Baslow. The Haddon Hall fishery downstream, which I have not fished, is available through the Peacock Hotel at Rowsley.

TEIFI

The stretches described are controlled by the Tregaron Angling Association and the Llandyssul Angling Association. Permits for the waters of both fisheries are available in local shops.

PIDDLE

Fishing can be obtained by staying at the Tolpuddle Trout Fishery, either in self-catering cottages or bed and breakfast. Contact Richard Slocock at Lawrence's Farm, Tolpuddle, Dorset.

TAMAR AND TRIBUTARIES

Fishing available on about twenty miles of river to guests at the Arundell Arms, Lifton, Devon.

TORRIDGE

Fishing available to guests at the Half Moon Inn, Sheepwash, Devon, or in the self-catering accommodation at Little Warham, Beaford, Winkleigh, Devon.

PENNSYLVANIA

Most of the fishing described can be obtained by holders of a Pennsylvania Fish and Game Commission licence, available at tackle shops. On the Rolling Rock fishery a day permit was necessary and the Spruce Creek fishing was at a private club.

ROCKY MOUNTAINS

Fishing on most waters is available to holders of the appropriate state Fish and Game Commission licence. Fishing on the Firehole and other waters in

Yellowstone National Park is included in the entry permit, but a separate fishing permit at no extra cost had to be obtained. For Armstrong Spring Creek a permit was obtained from DePuys Ranch.

KERRY

All waters fished were entirely free, but if access makes it necessary to cross obviously private land, it is a courtesy to ask permission.

The ownership of fisheries does change from time to time, so it is always advisable to check before making a long journey.

FURTHER READING

*T*HE BOOK THAT FIRST FIRED my imagination and made me want to take up fly fishing was *Mr Crabtree Goes Fishing*, Bernard Venables's wonderful volume based on his comic strip series in the *Daily Mirror*. The chapters on fly fishing for chub and dace made me look at the coarse fish that I was catching at that time in a new light, and the section on fly fishing for trout opened up the possibility of seeking an entirely new species. Then I read *A Fisherman's Testament* by the same author, and the evocative chapters on fishing the Kennet in Berkshire and the Coln in Gloucestershire meant that it would be only a matter of time before I cast my first fly on a trout stream.

I suppose that it was acquiring an old copy of *Where to Fish*, the 1951–2 edition by William Luscombe, that first made me aware of the world of waters waiting to be fished, and since then I have always looked for books and articles that give details of exciting places to fish for trout. Learning that the closing passage of Sir Edward Grey's *Fly Fishing* referred to the Suir in Ireland motivated my first visit to that river, and long before moving to Devon it was the chapters on fishing for brown trout on the moors in Kenneth Dawson's *Salmon and Trout on Moorland Streams* that attracted me to the streams of Dartmoor. My interest in the Dartmoor rivers was also kindled by *The Angler and the Trout* by Huish Edye.

Soon after taking up fly fishing, I was given the three volumes of *The Art of Angling* edited by Kenneth Mansfield and, at that stage, found three chapters particularly useful. They were on river trouting with sunk fly by Tom Ivens, dry-fly fishing on rain-fed rivers by the Reverend Edward Powell and chalkstream fishing by C. F. Walker. The latter wrote numerous books on fly fishing and also edited the original *Complete Fly Fisher*. He is probably best known for his *Chalk Stream Flies* and *Lake Flies and Their Imitation*, but for a pleasant read I often pick up his *Brown Trout and Dry Fly*.

Although Skues must be looked upon as the father of nymph fishing, the essential reading on modern nymph fishing must be *Nymphs and the Trout* by Frank Sawyer and *Nymph Fishing in Practice* by Oliver Kite. The latter is brought to life by the chapters on outings in search of trout on a variety of rivers.

When I started to take an interest in identifying the insects upon which trout feed, I turned first to the *Anglers' Entomology* by J. R. Harris and *Trout Fly Recognition* by John Goddard, and learned much from both books. A much more compact guide to fly life is now available in John Goddard's *Waterside Guide*.

While the sector of trout fly fishing which has developed fastest in Britain in recent years, and inspired the most books, has been reservoir fishing from bank and boat, on the other side of the Atlantic the picture has been very different. There, fly fishing for trout is essentially stream fishing and there has been a rich flowering of literature on the subject. Authors such as Marinaro, Flick, Schwiebert, Brooks, Swisher, Richards, Caucci, Nastasi, Jorgensen and others have introduced readers to many new concepts of fishing and fly tying, and any river trout fisherman should have a selection of their works.

I first read *A Modern Dry Fly Code* by Vince Marinaro many years ago and realized for the first time the importance of terrestrial insects, which applies as much on my local Devon rivers as on his limestone streams in Pennsylvania. I read *The Trout and the Stream* by Charles E. Brooks soon after it was published in 1974 and his chapters on the fishing around Yellowstone National Park were instrumental in motivating me to fish there. This book also has much to offer on fishing techniques, fly patterns and conservation. My fly tying has certainly improved from constant references to *Modern Fly Dressing for the Practical Angler* by Poul Jorgensen, *Master Fly-Tying Guide* edited by Art Flick, and *Fly-Tying Methods* by Darrel Martin. Two anthologies which bring together the work of many American writers on fly fishing are *The Masters of the Nymph* and *The Masters of the Dry Fly*.

I have to declare an interest in three fishing books to which I have contributed – *West Country Fly Fishing* edited by Anne Voss Bark, *The Haig Guide to Trout Fishing in Britain* edited by David Barr, and the new edition of *The Complete Fly Fisher* edited by Peter Lapsley. However, I frequently refer to these books to benefit from the words of the other contributors.

And then there are those books which I pick up just for a pleasant read. These include classics such as *Where the Bright Waters Meet* by H. Plunket Greene and *Going Fishing* by Negley Farson, as well as more recent works like Howard Marshall's *Reflections on a River* and the collection of Conrad Voss Bark's angling contributions to *The Times* in *A Fly on the Water*. As I look over the spines of the fishing books in my collection, I realize how many other enjoyable and informative books I have overlooked – *A Fly Fisher's Life* by Charles Ritz, *The Trout and the Fly* by Brian Clarke and John Goddard, and that indispensable guide to standard fly patterns, *A Dictionary of Trout Flies* by Courtney Williams.

INDEX